starting out in
backgammon

PAUL LAMFORD

Published by Everyman Publishers plc, London

First published 2001 by Everyman Publishers plc, Gloucester Mansions, 140A Shaftesbury Avenue, London WC2H 8HD

British Library Cataloguing-in-Publication Data
A catalogue record of this book is available from the British Library.

ISBN 1 85744 282 2

Distributed in North America by The Globe Pequot Press, P O Box 480, 246 Goose Lane, Guilford, CT 06437-0480.

All other sales enquiries should be directed to Mindsports, Everyman Publishers plc, Gloucester Mansions, 140A Shaftesbury Avenue, London WC2H 8HD
Tel: 020 7539 7600 Fax: 020 7379 4060
email: dan@everyman.uk.com website: www.everyman.uk.com

To Claudine Murphy

The Everyman Mindsports series was designed and developed by First Rank Publishing

Typeset by Games and Pastimes Consultancy, London (gampas@aol.com)
Production by Book Production Services
Printed and bound in Great Britain by The Cromwell Press Ltd, Trowbridge, Wiltshire

Contents

Introduction

Backgammon is a race game, and is probably descended from very old games such as the Egyptian *senet* or the Indian *parcheesi*, although game boards with a slight resemblance to backgammon were found in Ur, and date back around five thousand years. The game as we know it was mentioned in Cotton's *The Compleat Gamester* of 1674, although there were certainly differences:

> 'If your Tables be clear before your Adverſaries men be come in, that's a *Back-Gammon*, which is three; but if you thus go off with Doublets it is four.'

The game was analysed in 1743 in Hoyle's *A Short Treatise on the Game of Back' Gammon*. It underwent its most recent change in the 1920s with the addition of the doubling cube.

Since 1967 backgammon has had an annual World Championship, which started in Las Vegas and the Bahamas, but moved to its present home in Monte Carlo in 1976. There are now about twenty major international tournaments each year, and regular domestic events in the 100 or so countries in which backgammon is played.

How popular is the game? One good way of assessing a game's popularity is the Internet, and there are about 100,000 players in total on the Internet servers. It is estimated that, in the USA, about three million play regularly, while in the UK around three quarters of a million do so. Most of these think of backgammon as a game of luck. I hope that after reading this book you will be convinced that it involves considerable skill.

The author acknowledges the assistance in the preparation of this book of the computer programs Snowie and Jellyfish. Particular thanks are due to Simon Gasquoine and Stefanie Rohan for editing, proofreading, and checking positions. Byron Jacobs also deserves thanks for suggesting this title and the companion one on bridge. The author accepts responsibility for any errors and would welcome comments or corrections sent to him at gampas@aol.com.

We have adopted the convention of referring to White, or 'the player' as 'he' and Black, or 'the opponent' as 'she'.

Chapter One

The Basics

How the Game is Played

Backgammon is a race game. Each player has 15 checkers and moves them according to the roll of two dice. The main object is to remove all 15 checkers from the board before the opponent. The game is played on a board marked with 24 spiked playing segments known as points. The starting position is shown in diagram 1. (One can also set up the starting position with the mirror image, i.e. White's home board on his left.)

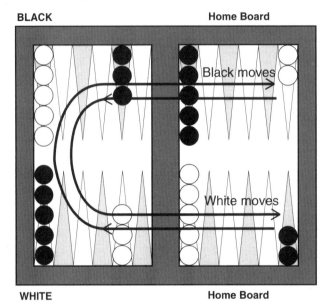

BLACK   Home Board

Black moves

White moves

WHITE   Home Board   Diag. 1

Each player uses two standard dice, with the numbers one to six on the faces. To begin the game, each player rolls one die on the half of the board to his right. The player who rolls the higher number makes the opening move of the game (if the same number is rolled then both dice must be rolled again until they are different). The player with the higher number moves one checker, in the direction shown by the arrows in the above diagram, the number of pips shown on one die, and the same or another checker the number of pips shown on the other die, again in the direction shown by the arrows. The direction of play is always towards a player's home board and the two home boards are shown in the above diagram. The dice are picked up and the opponent then rolls two dice in the half of the board on his right to decide the roll for his first play. Thereafter the roll alternates.

The Moves of the Checkers

A checker may not move onto a point occupied by two or more of the opponent's checkers. If the same checker is used for both parts of a move, then the first part of the move must also be to a point not occupied by two or more of the opponent's checkers. Let us look at the first few moves of a typical game. White rolls a four and Black rolls a three in the starting position. White has several possible moves and might decide to make the move shown in diagram 2:

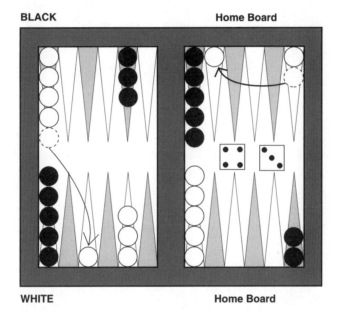

BLACK **Home Board**

WHITE **Home Board** **Diag. 2**

Hitting

If a checker moves onto a point occupied by a single checker of the opponent, the latter is 'hit' and is immediately placed on the bar (the central strip dividing the two halves of the board). The hitting checker replaces the hit checker on that point. A solitary checker which can be hit is known as a 'blot'. Continuing from the above diagram, Black rolls a six and a three in reply to the opening 4-3. She can hit the white checker as shown in diagram 3 overleaf.

If one or more checkers have been hit and are on the bar, then such checkers must be entered before any other checkers may be moved. This is done by rolling a number corresponding to a point in the opponent's home board not occupied by two or more

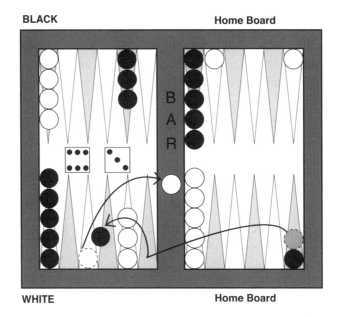

Diag. 3

of the opponent's checkers. Say the game continues with White rolling a 6-1, as shown below. The home boards are indicated, and the points in Black's home board are numbered from one to six. As the six-point is occupied by two or more of Black's checkers, the first move must be to enter the checker from the bar with the one. With the six, White continues with the same checker:

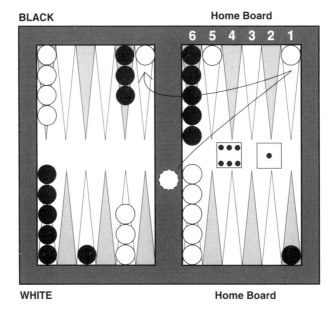

Diag. 4

Doubles

After the opening roll, if the numbers rolled on the two dice are the same, the player is said to have rolled a double. When a double is rolled, the player makes four separate moves of the number shown, one or more of which can be with the same checker. Again all moves or parts of moves must be to points not occupied by two or more of the opponent's checkers, and up to four checkers may be hit and placed on the bar.

Incomplete or Forfeited Moves

A player must move both numbers on the dice if it is possible to do so. Often a player cannot move at all. This most frequently happens when he is on the bar and the numbers rolled correspond to points that the opponent has made in his board. Sometimes the player is not on the bar, but there is no legal way to play either of the numbers on the dice. In all of these cases, the player misses a turn and the opponent rolls. If a player can play only one number on the dice, but not both, then any move can be made for that number.

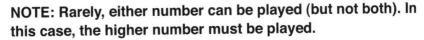 **NOTE: Rarely, either number can be played (but not both). In this case, the higher number must be played.**

Bearing Off

When a player has all of his remaining checkers in his home board, then he may begin to remove checkers. A checker may be removed from the point (using the same numbering system as diagram 4) corresponding to a number shown on one die. If the number rolled on either die corresponds to a vacant point, and a player has no checker on a higher-numbered point, then a checker must be borne off from the highest-numbered point. If, however, the player does have a checker on a higher-numbered point, then a move must be made within the player's board without bearing off. It should be noted that there is no obligation to bear off a checker, and on occasions it may be better to move a checker within the board, even though a checker could be borne off. In diagram 5 White rolls a 6-3. With the six he must bear off a checker from the five-point, as he has no checker on the six-point. With the three, he is unable to bear off a checker, as the three-point is empty and he still has checkers on higher-numbered points. He must therefore move the three from the five- or four-point as he prefers. One other important point is that if a player has a checker (or checkers)

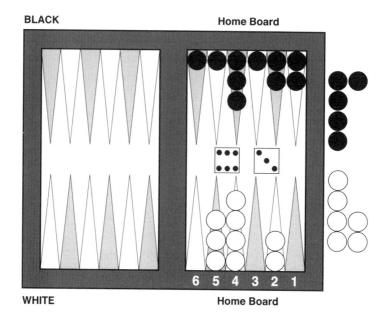

Diag. 5

hit after he has started bearing off, then all such checkers must re-enter the opponent's home board and move round to the player's home board before the bear-off can resume.

Scoring

The scoring of the game is important. The first player to remove all his checkers is the winner. If the loser has removed at least one checker, the winner gets one point. If the loser has not removed any checkers, then a gammon is scored. This is worth two points. Finally, if the loser still has a checker in the winner's home board or on the bar, and has not removed any checkers when the winner removes his final checker, then a backgammon is scored. This is worth three points.

 NOTE: There are some variants of backgammon in which the starting position, rules and scoring are different

A number of these can be found and played on the Internet server at www.vog.ru. The above rules apply in all backgammon events under the auspices of the World Backgammon Federation.

Furthermore, as we shall see in Chapter Four, the scores can be increased by the use of a doubling cube.

Notation

Up until now we have avoided introducing the reader to backgammon notation, preferring to use arrows to show the moves. However, as we discuss more complicated principles we shall need to use the notation to refer to moves and to the 24 points on the board. The backgammon board is numbered from 1 to 24 **from each player's point of view.** Thus White's one-point is Black's 24-point. The numbering of the board from White's point of view is as follows:

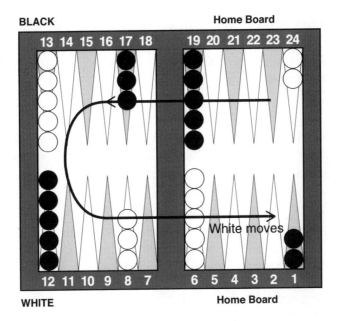

Diag. 6

A move is shown from the point of view of the player on roll. If, in the starting position, White rolls a four and a three, then this roll is notated as 4-3. If White moves as shown in diagram 2, the move is notated **1   4-3: 24/20 13/10** (the 1 is the move number). An oblique is used to separate the point of departure and point of arrival. In this book the roll is shown with a hyphen between the two numbers. If the same checker moves one or more times, then only the initial point of departure and final point of arrival are shown, unless this creates an ambiguity as to whether a checker has been hit en route, in which case the separate parts of the move need to be notated. If a checker is hit, then an asterisk is placed after the move. Thus

Black's reply in diagram 3 would be notated 6-3: 24/15*. Here it is not necessary to indicate whether Black began with 24/18 or 24/21 as the first part of the move. The game record would now look like this:

1   4-3:   24/20 13/10   6-3:   24/15*

The above information is sufficient for anyone to reach the same position after one move by each side, and this simple notation, which is universal, allows backgammon enthusiasts to replay, on their boards, games from World Championships and other top events.

Other abbreviations

When a hit checker enters from the bar, then the point of departure is shown as 'b'. Thus in diagram 4, White's second move is shows as follows:

2   6-1:   b/18

Note that is not necessary to indicate that the checker entered on White's 24-point (Black's one-point) as there is no ambiguity. Even if there were (say the roll were 4-3, also played b/18) there would be no need to indicate whether the checker had entered on the 21- or 22-point, as the same position is reached. However, if Black had had a checker on her four-point and White had hit this as the first part of the move, then one would need to notate the move as b/21*/18.

When a checker is borne off, then the point of arrival is shown as 'o'. Thus, in diagram 5 on page 10, White bears off a checker from his five-point and moves a checker from his four-point to his one-point. The move is notated: 6-3: 5/o 4/1. If a move which does not bear off a checker must be played first, then it is shown first.

Sometimes readers will find the numbers 25 and 0 used instead of 'b' and 'o' respectively, particularly in computer records of games played on the Internet. This book has preferred the traditional notation using 'b' and 'o', but readers should have no problem coping with the alternative notation.

When a double is rolled and two or more checkers move between the same points, then the move is notated by putting a number in brackets corresponding to the number of identical moves played. Thus, from diagram 4 on page 8, if Black rolled 3-3 in reply to White's move, then she could move one checker from her 13-point to hit the white checker on her seven-point and two checkers from her eight-point to her five-point, hitting another white checker in the process. This move would be notated: **3-3: 13/7* 8/5(2)***. Our move record to date is now as follows:

1	4-3:	24/20 13/10	6-3:	24/15*
2	6-1:	b/18	3-3:	13/7* 8/5(2)*

Additional Information

a) The reader may have seen a cube with faces showing the numbers 2, 4, 8, 16, 32 and 64. This is known as the doubling cube and will be explained in Chapter Four.

b) The checkers that have been borne off are shown to the right of the board in the diagrams. In addition, the player to move is shown by an arrow to the right of the board. In the diagrams on the next page it is White to move.

c) There are one or two commonly-held misconceptions about the rules. Firstly, a player may have any number of checkers on a point. Secondly, a player may not re-roll if he or she does not like the opening roll. Finally, there is no obligation to hit a checker or bear off a checker, provided that the earlier rule about playing both rolls of the dice if possible, or the higher number if only one can be played, is followed.

d) There are some important rules relating to the procedures of the game. For a roll to be valid, both dice must come to rest on the playing surface on the roller's right, and not on top of one of the checkers. If they do not, the dice are said to be cocked and must be rolled again. If a player moves illegally, the opponent can accept the incorrect move or make the player move correctly.

e) The traditional rule in tournaments is that you may change your mind about your move until you have picked up your dice. It is poor etiquette, however, to keep moving your checkers around.

Solutions to all exercises begin on page 118.

Exercise 1: Play the two moves on page 13 from the starting position, beginning with White. You should reach the following position, with White to move. If not, re-read the section on notation.

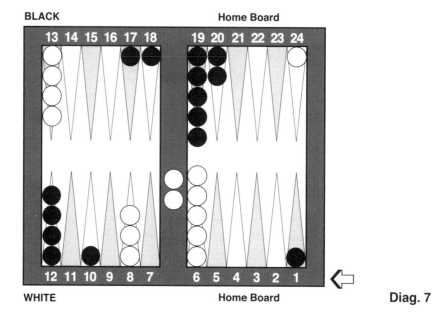

Diag. 7

Exercise 2: White rolls a 5-3 in the following position; how many different legal moves are there?

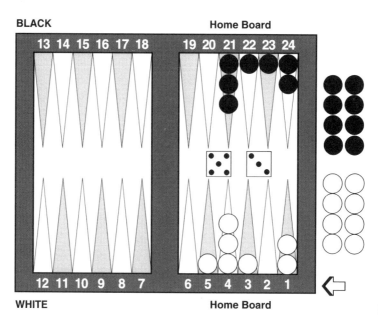

Diag. 8

Chapter Two

Early Strategy

- **Blocking the Opponent**
- **The Aims of the Opening**
- **The Important Points**
- **Hitting Checkers**

Blocking the Opponent

If the only strategy in backgammon were to move the checkers around the board as quickly as possible, then it would not be a particularly interesting game. However, each player should combine the aim of bringing his own checkers into his home board with a strategy of blocking the opponent.

TIP: The way to impede the opponent's progress is to build a series of points in a row

As we saw in the first chapter, the opponent cannot move onto a point occupied by two or more of your checkers, and several such points in a row form a formidable obstacle. For example:

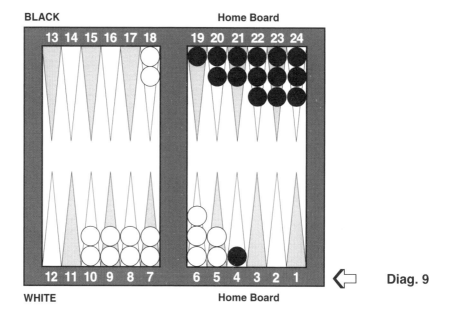

Diag. 9

Black has moved all but one of her checkers into her home board, and, at first glance, would appear to be ahead in the race to take off checkers. However, White has formed a blockade of six points in a row on his side of the board and has trapped a black checker behind it. Black will not be able to move that checker until White lifts this blockade. Such a blockade is known as a prime, and, as this one consists of six consecutive points, it is called a six-prime. A prime with a gap in it is known as a broken prime. The term 'prime' is normally used only for four or more consecutive points with no more than one gap. White's winning chances in diagram 9 are around 90%. His strategy will be to retain six points in a row while hitting the black checker at the edge of the prime. Unless White is very unlucky, his six-prime will roll to the right, and the black checker should eventually be closed out, with White making all six points in his board. White will thus begin bearing off first.

The Aims of the Opening

In the early stages there is much jockeying for position. Each player starts the game with four occupied points, but two of these have five checkers each, more than are needed. In the early stages the players attempt to make new blocking points, using these surplus checkers. For example, let us look at an opening roll of 3-1. This is regarded as the strongest opening roll, even though it contains only four pips. The correct way to play it is as in diagram 10:

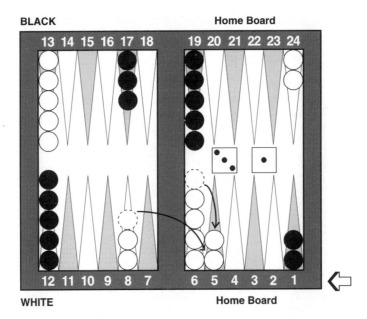

Diag. 10

White moves one checker from his eight-point to his five-point and one checker from his six-point to his five-point. This move is notated **8/5 6/5**. The new point which White has made prevents Black from moving a four with a checker on White's one-point. Of course not all rolls allow you to make a new point.

Indeed, of the opening rolls, only five allow you to do so (6-1, 3-1, 4-2, 5-3 and 6-4), and the last of these is as often as not played without making a new point. When you roll anything else you will either have to move a checker from one occupied point to another or move a checker to a vacant point.

TIP: Generally, in the opening, it pays to take a few risks by moving checkers to unoccupied points in an effort to make new blocking points

Although the opponent may hit a lone checker and send it to the bar, in the early stages this is not serious. The correct way to play most opening rolls involves leaving one or more checkers exposed.

The Important Points

Sometimes we have a choice of points to make in the opening. The most important points on the board are each player's five-point. If we can make our five-point we usually should. If we can make the opponent's five-point we also usually should, as this both makes a new point of our own and prevents the opponent from making it.

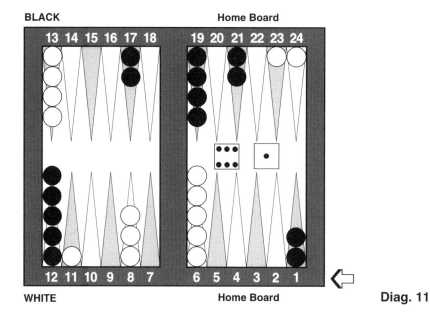

Diag. 11

This position has occurred after one move by each side. White rolled a 2-1 which he played 24/23 13/11 and Black replied with a 4-2, which she played 8/4 6/4, making her four-point. White has now rolled a 6-1 and can make either the seven-point with 13/7 8/7 or the five-point with 11/5 6/5. The latter is stronger.

TIP: The five-point is the most important point on the board

The value of the other points can vary, but usually the seven-point (also known as the bar-point) and the four-point are about equal, as are the eight-point and three-point. Generally the nine-point is better than the two-point. Whether to make one's own point or to make the same point on the opponent's side of the board depends on the priorities in the position.

Hitting Checkers

As we saw in Chapter One, if an opponent's checker is hit, it is placed on the bar and must re-enter before any other checker can be moved. Does this mean that it is always correct to hit an opposing checker? By no means. Firstly, the location of the opposing checker is an important factor. If you hit an opposing checker in the opponent's half of the board, that checker is sent back much further than if you hit a checker in your home board. However, other factors come into play in the opening. It is often correct to hit the opponent's checker when it is occupying a point you want to make. For example:

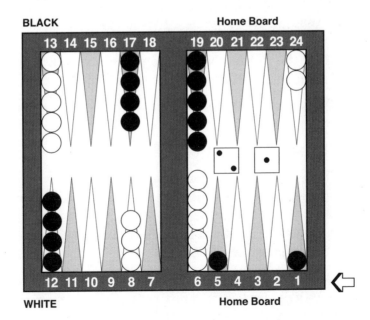

Diag. 12

Black rolled an opening 5-4 and played 13/8 24/20. As we shall see later this is one of the best ways for Black to play this roll. Now White rolls a 2-1. I have seen beginners play moves like 24/21 or, even worse, 8/6 24/23. They are terrified to leave loose checkers on their side of the board. However, the correct play is 13/11 6/5* leading to the following position:

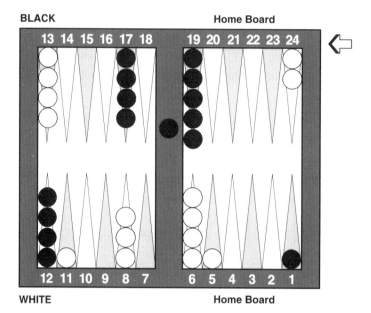

BLACK   Home Board

13 14 15 16 17 18   19 20 21 22 23 24

12 11 10 9 8 7   6 5 4 3 2 1

WHITE   Home Board   **Diag. 13**

It is true that Black may well now hit the checker on White's five-point. However, being hit in the opening is not a disaster, and if Black does not hit, White has an excellent chance to cover the checker on his five-point next roll. Black is a slight favourite to hit, but the risk is worth taking.

There is an oft-quoted adage in backgammon which should stand the beginner in good stead:

TIP: When in doubt, hit!

However, there are some exceptions. Usually it is wrong to hit on your own one-point (also known as the ace-point) or two-point (often called the deuce-point) in the opening. Hitting two checkers is usually right and again there is a proverb: 'Two on the bar is better by far!'

One other aspect of the opening to mention is that you often have a choice between hitting a checker and making a new point. Usually hitting is stronger.

Exercise 3: How should White play 4-3 in the following position?

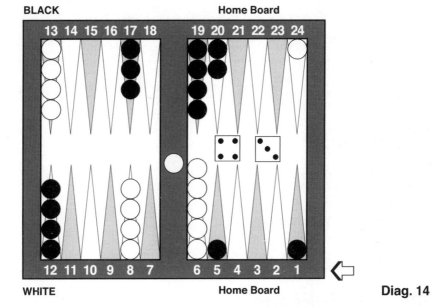

Diag. 14

Exercise 4: How should White play 6-4 in the following position?

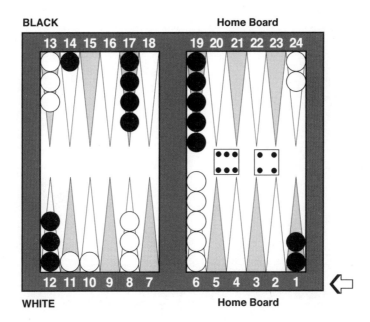

Diag. 15

Chapter Three

Opening Moves and Replies

Basic Principles

There are 15 possible opening rolls (6-5, 6-4, 6-3, 6-2, 6-1, 5-4, 5-3, 5-2, 5-1, 4-3, 4-2, 4-1, 3-2, 3-1, 2-1), as it is not possible to roll a double for the opening roll.

TIP: With each move you have to consider offence and defence — the competing objectives of escaping your back checkers and blocking your opponent's checkers

Let us look at some general guidelines for the opening stage of the game:

a) You do not want a sixth checker on any point unless there is no sensible alternative.

b) If you can escape a back checker to safety, it is usually right to do so.

c) Splitting the back checkers so that they occupy two different points is usually a good idea early on as it gives extra flexibility. After the opponent has made several new points it becomes more dangerous.

d) Bringing one or two checkers down from the 13-point (also known as the mid-point) to the nine-, ten- or 11-points is usually a good idea, unless the opponent has a checker six pips or fewer away from the checker you bring down. Such checkers are known as builders and can be used to make new points.

e) Usually it is right to hit an opposing checker on your five- or four-point. It is seldom right to hit on your three-, two- or ace-point, unless you are hitting two checkers, or you have made extra home-board points already.

f) Running a back checker out to the 14-, 15- or 16-point is playable if there is no reasonable alternative. If the checker is not hit you gain; if it is hit you suffer.

Point-Making Rolls

While there is disagreement amongst top experts on a few of the opening rolls, the following four rolls would be played by all good players in the same way. In each case they make a new point without any risk.

a) **3-1**. Make the five-point with 8/5 6/5:

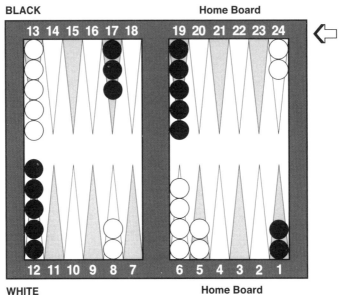

Diag. 16

b) **4-2**. Make the four-point with 8/4 6/4:

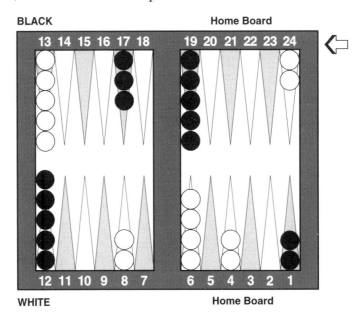

Diag. 17

These are the two best opening rolls, allowing you to use one of the spares on the six-point to make a new point. The third-best opening roll is:

c) **6-1**. Make the seven-point with 13/7 8/7:

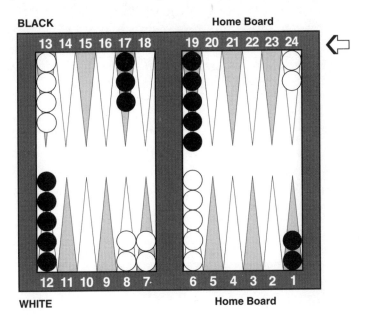

Diag. 18

It is worth mentioning at this point that former World Champion Paul Magriel experimented with the bizarre 13/7 6/5 and won games because of the surprise effect. In the words of John McEnroe: 'You cannot be serious.'

d) **5-3**. Make the three-point with 8/3 6/3:

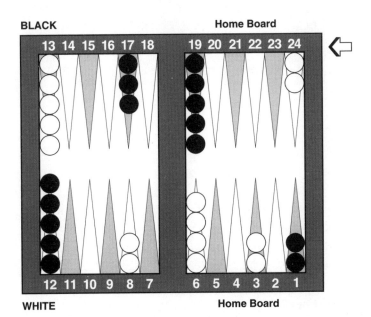

Diag. 19

An opening 5-3 used to be played by bringing two checkers down from the 13-point with 13/8 13/10, but modern experts prefer to make the three-point. Players who learnt backgammon in the sixties and seventies often bring down the two builders, and there is no clear evidence that there is anything wrong with their strategy now.

Running Plays

There are a couple of big rolls with which you take an early lead in the race to bring your checkers home. These are usually played by running one of the checkers from the 24-point.

e) **6-4**. Run one checker with 24/14:

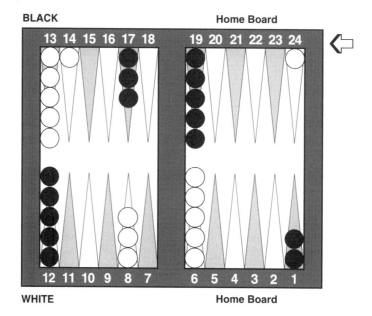

Diag. 20

The above is the traditional play of an opening 6-4 and is still the choice of many top experts. However two other possibilities come into consideration. 24/18 13/9 is very similar to the major splitting plays below and is a good alternative. 8/2 6/2 used to be regarded as a beginner's error but, with the advent of stronger and stronger backgammon software programs, it has started to be taken seriously. The move makes a new home-board point and leaves no loose checkers. It also makes some replies containing a one awkward to play. Top players often try the play.

f) **6-5**. Run one checker with 24/13:

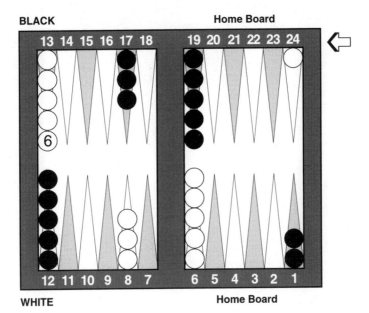

Diag. 21

This is a case of one principle (escaping a back checker) taking priority over a less vital one (avoiding stacking six checkers on the same-point). The move brings a back checker to safety and avoids leaving any blots. The alternatives are also unattractive from a constructive standpoint.

Major Splits

There are two types of split one can make with the back checkers: major and minor. The major splits involve moving a back checker to a point which both you and the opponent would like to make, immediately causing a confrontation. These include a couple of rolls with a six, one with a four, and a couple with a three. In each case the other number is used to bring a checker down from the mid-point. The idea is to seize one of the points the opponent would like to make.

NOTE: A point made in the opponent's board, or on her seven-point (also known as the bar-point), is called an anchor

Your 18-point, 20-point or 21-point is known as an advanced anchor. As we shall see later, moving up the back checkers to obtain an advanced anchor is desirable. It is much harder for the opponent to build a blocking prime in front of it.

g) **6-3**. Split with 24/18 and bring a builder down with 13/10:

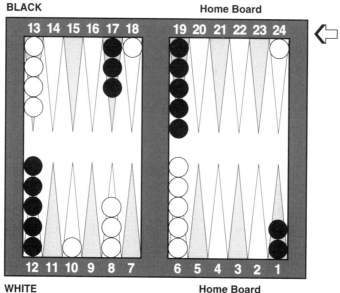

Diag. 22

h) **6-2**. Split with 24/18 and bring a builder down with 13/11:

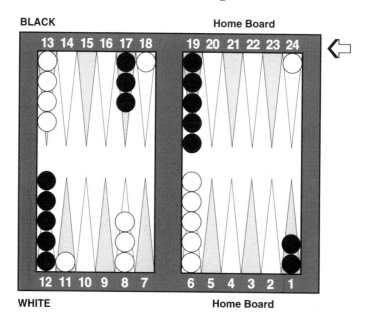

Diag. 23

The above two moves are very similar. The aim is to try to make White's 18-point. It is true that Black can hit this checker with any six or one, but White may then hit back from the bar with almost any six or seven.

i) **5-4**. Split to the opponent's five-point with 24/20 and bring a checker down from the mid-point with 13/8:

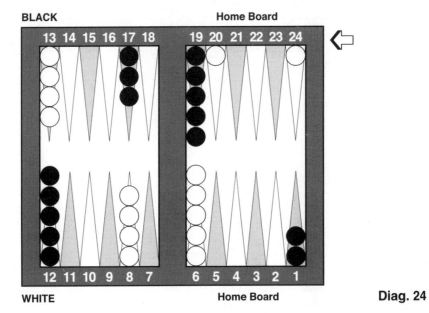

Diag. 24

j) **4-3**. Split to the opponent's four-point with 24/21 and bring a builder down from the mid-point with 13/9. There are several plays that are nearly as good here.

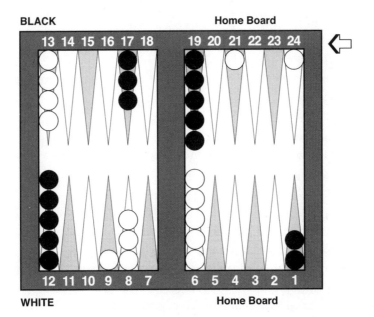

Diag. 25

k) **3-2**. Split to the opponent's four-point with 24/21 and bring a builder down from the mid-point with 13/11:

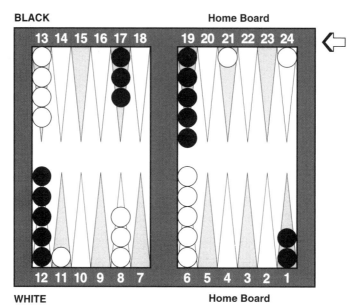

Diag. 26

Several of the above rolls are played differently by leading experts. Certainly the last three, i, j and k, are often played by bringing down two builders from the mid-point and these older plays may well be equally good. Backgammon openings go in and out of fashion, and you may want to experiment with other plays to find the one which suits you.

Minor Splits

There are three plays, each containing a one, which used to be played universally by moving a checker from the six-point to the five-point with the ace, known as slotting the five-point. They are 5-1, 4-1 and 2-1. The advent of very strong backgammon-playing computer programs allowed leading experts to test the theory that leaving a loose checker, exposed to any four, or combination totalling four, was worth the risk in an attempt to make the important five-point. In general, the computers came back with the answer that it was not. As a consequence players now usually prefer to use the ace to split the back checkers with 24/23 (the 'minor split') either with the opening roll or with the reply to the opening roll.

l) **5-1**. Split with 24/23 and bring another checker to the eight-point with 13/8:

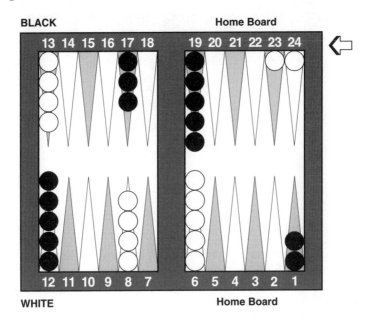

Diag. 27

m) **4-1**. Split with 24/23 and bring down a builder from the mid-point with 13/9. The nine-point is the best place to have a builder for making a new inner-board point:

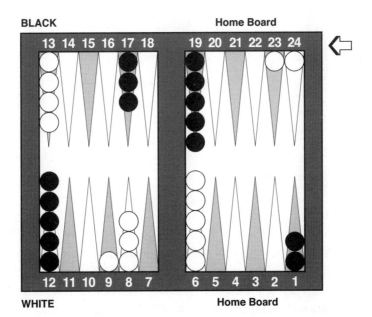

Diag. 28

n) **2-1**. Split with 24/23 and bring down a builder with 13/11:

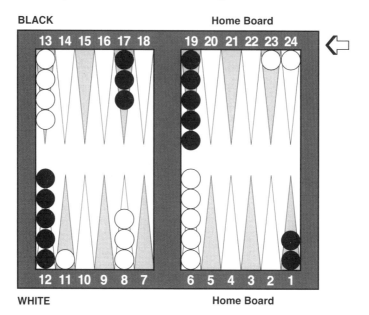

Diag. 29

o) **5-2**. Split with 24/22 and bring a checker down with 13/8:

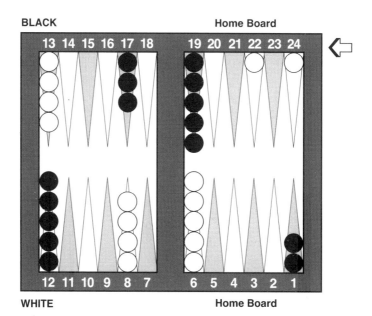

Diag. 30

This concludes our recommendations for the fifteen opening rolls. Readers comparing this book with a backgammon primer of the 1970s will note the differences. There is a table summarising the best moves at the end of this chapter.

Replies to Opening Moves

There are 21 possible rolls after each of the 15 opening moves, so it can be seen that the number of opening positions is quite large. Indeed, someone once calculated that there are more possible positions in backgammon than in chess. We will not confuse the reader with a mass of data here, but instead give practical guidelines:

Doubles

1) There are six doubles which need to be considered, and the best play in each case will depend on the opponent's first move and how it was played:

1a) **6-6**. If you can make both bar-points you should. If your opponent has made her bar-point (with a 6/1), then make your bar-point and your two-point with 13/7(2) 8/2(2).

1b) **5-5**. If your opponent has split her back checkers, either with a major split or a minor split, then you should attack with 8/3(2) 6/1*(2). This primitive but very effective strategy is the start of a blitz, which will be looked at in more detail in Chapter Eight. In diagram 31, White has played an opening 6-2 24/18 13/11 and Black's reply of 5-5 has put a checker on the bar, beginning a blitz:

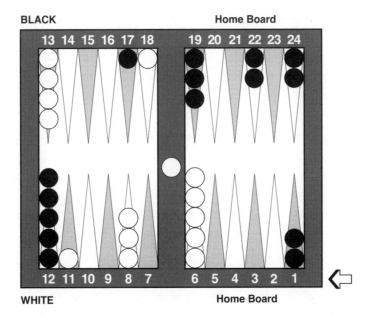

Diag. 31

If your opponent has not split her back checkers, then you should just make the three-point with 13/3(2).

1c) **4-4**. The correct play depends on whether you can hit any checkers. If you can, you should, and then use the other fours to make a new point, which may be your nine-point or your 20-point. If you cannot hit any checkers, play 24/20(2) 13/9(2).

WARNING: It is usually not worth giving up the eight-point to make the four-point, unless you are pointing on the opponent

1d) **3-3**. Again the best play depends on whether you can hit any checkers and whether the opponent has made any new points. Usually you will make the 21-point and 10-point. If you are hitting a checker in your home board, you would make the five- and three-points.

1e) **2-2**. Usually you make the four-point with 6/4(2) and 11-point with 13/11(2), or 22-point with 24/22(2). If the opponent has slotted her five-point, however, then you hit with 24/20* and make the four-point with 6/4(2). Do not use four twos to hit on the 16-point or three twos to hit on your bar-point.

1f) **1-1**. If your opponent has not split her back checkers, or she has split to your five-point or bar-point, then make your five-point and bar-point with 8/7(2) 6/5(2). If the opponent has split to your four-point, play 6/4*(2). Otherwise make the five-point with 6/5(2) and split at the back with 24/22.

Non-Doubles

These moves are often played in the same way as the opening rolls. We will mainly mention here when they should be played differently. We have retained the original lettering system, so that you may refer back to that recommendation:

a) **3-1** b) **4-2** c) **6-1** and d) **5-3**. These point-making rolls are generally played as for the opening rolls. There are a few exceptions. If you can hit a checker on the opponent's side of the board, or on your nine-, ten, or 11-point, then you should. However, do not vary from the original strategy to hit a checker on your seven-point.

e) **6-4** and f) **6-5**. These are generally played the same way, by running. An exception is that if your opponent has made a minor split with 24/23, then you should use a 6-4 to point on that checker with 8/2* 6/2.

g) **6-3**. If you can hit a checker on the opponent's side of the board or your own bar-point, do so. Generally you play as for the opening roll, except if your opponent has made a major split. In that case running with 24/15 is better, unless she has split to your four-point when you should hit with 13/4*.

h) **6-2**. Similarly, you should hit on your 16-point or your bar-point, five-point or four-point if possible. Otherwise play as for the opening roll.

i) **5-4**. Hit on the opponent's side of the board if you can; otherwise usually play as for the opening roll. If your opponent has brought two builders down from her mid-point, do not play 24/20; instead play 13/8 13/9.

j) **4-3**. Usually play as for the opening roll. If you can hit on your five-point or four-point you should, and if you can hit two checkers you should. Usually if you hit with one number, then you split at the back with the other number.

k) **3-2**. If you can hit two checkers then you should. If your opponent has split to her 21- or 22-point then this will be possible, so look out for this. Hit on your five-point or four-point if you can. Otherwise you should play as for the opening roll, unless your opponent has split to your bar-point, when 24/21 24/22 is better.

l) **5-1**. Usually play the normal move. If the opponent has split to your bar-point, then hit two checkers with 8/7* 6/1*. Hit on your five-point if your opponent has played 24/20.

m) **4-1**. Again, usually play as for the opening roll. If your opponent has split to your five-point then the double hit with 6/5* 5/1* is correct. If your opponent has split to your four-point, then you should hit with 8/4* and play 24/23.

n) **2-1**. If you can hit a checker (except on your three-point), then do so. Otherwise play the normal move, unless your opponent has played 24/16, when you should play 24/21.

o) **5-2**. Usually play the normal move. If you can hit on your four-point or 11-point with the two, then you should.

Overleaf there is a chart of the opening moves and a good alternative if one exists. These are based on assessments and roll-outs by the strongest commercially available backgammon program, Snowie 3.

Opening Roll	Best Play	Good Alternative
3-1	8/5 6/5	—
4-2	8/4 6/4	—
6-1	13/7 8/7	—
5-3	8/3 6/3	—
6-5	24/13	—
6-4	24/14	24/18 13/9
6-3	24/18 13/10	24/15
6-2	24/18 13/11	24/16
5-4	24/20 13/8	13/8 13/9
4-3	24/21 13/9	24/20 13/10
3-2	24/21 13/11	13/11 13/10
5-1	13/8 24/23	13/8 6/5
4-1	13/9 24/23	13/8
2-1	13/11 24/23	13/11 6/5
5-2	13/8 24/22	13/8 13/11

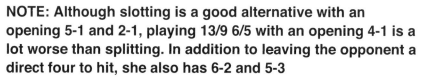

NOTE: Although slotting is a good alternative with an opening 5-1 and 2-1, playing 13/9 6/5 with an opening 4-1 is a lot worse than splitting. In addition to leaving the opponent a direct four to hit, she also has 6-2 and 5-3

In five cases, there is no good alternative. There is sometimes a third option, however. In particular 8/2 6/2 with a 6-4 is fine and leads to an interesting game. Also 13/9 13/10 is fine with a 4-3. Finally 13/8 for a 3-2 shares a psychological benefit with 13/8 for a 4-1. It gives your opponent the wrong impression that you are a weak player and know nothing about making new points!

One other factor to bear in mind is the strength of the opponent. Generally the slotting plays with an ace lead to more complicated positions, and should be preferred against a weaker player. In addition, bringing down builders from the mid-point tends to lead to priming games, as covered in Chapter Seven. These types of game are usually more difficult to play, and therefore ideal for the stronger player. If you are the weaker player, then you should avoid slotting and seek a less-complicated running game.

Exercise 5: How would you play a 3-2 in reply to your opponent's 3-2 in the following position?

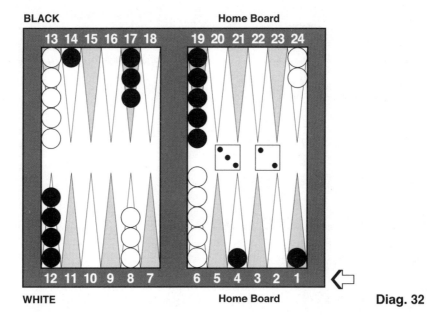

Diag. 32

Exercise 6: How would you play a 3-1 in reply to your opponent's 6-2 in the following position?

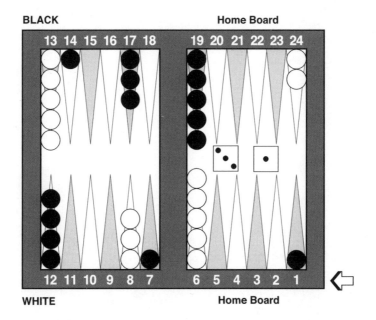

Diag. 33

Chapter Four

The Doubling Cube

- How it is used
- The 25% rule
- The Jacoby Rule
- Redoubles
- PRAT: Position, Race and Threats
- Too Good

How it is used

You may have seen a type of die with the numbers 2, 4, 8, 16, 32, and 64 on its faces. This is the doubling cube, which was invented in the USA in the 1920s. It is used to increase the number of points at stake in a backgammon game.

We say points, because the cube is of equal importance in games played for money as in games played for fun. However, for there to be any purpose in using the cube in the latter, one must be playing a match up to a set number of points. On the Internet, for example, the author often plays matches of five, seven, or even 11 points for no financial stake. The doubling cube usually plays a major part in these matches.

At any stage prior to rolling the dice, a player may make an initial offer of the cube. He places it, with the face showing the number two uppermost, on the half of the board on his right, as shown in diagram 34. The opponent either accepts, in which case the points scored will be doubled, or declines, in which case the person offering the cube wins one point. Take the following position, which we saw in the previous chapter. This time, Black is on roll. White has rolled a number which did not enter, and Black offered a double:

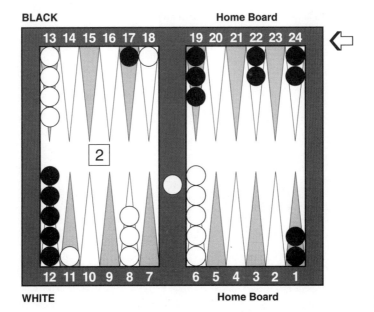

Diag. 34

This is an excellent offer of the doubling cube by Black, even though the game is only a few moves old. White has to decide whether to accept. It is extremely marginal, but White should do so even though he is a big underdog in the game. This chapter is concerned with the criteria for making these sorts of decisions.

The 25% rule

The beginner is mystified by the cube. The impression of most players new to the game is that they should double with any advantage, and refuse the cube if they are an underdog. However this is not the case. An approximate benchmark for deciding whether to accept a cube is that you should do so if you would win the game about 25% of the time.

TIP: If you prefer to think in terms of odds, you can accept a cube when you are no worse than 3-1 against

For example, a game which has been level throughout, and has therefore seen no cube turn, might reach the following position:

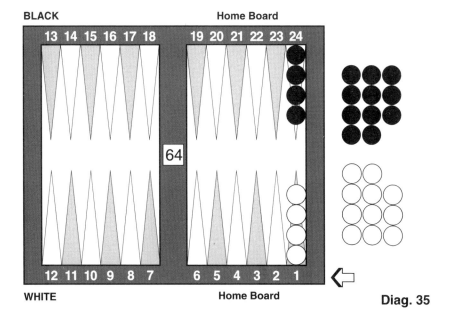

Diag. 35

White is on roll and wins if he rolls a double, or if neither player gets a double next roll. One sixth of rolls are doubles, so White wins 1/6 + (5/6 x 5/6) times, or 31 times in 36.

White should offer the cube on 2 and Black should pass. She is winning only five times in 36, which is about 14%, much less than the required 25% of the time. If the game is played for one pound a point, then Black would lose a pound by refusing the cube, but more than one pound by accepting (about £1.44 on average). If Black accepts, it is the equivalent of her placing a bet on a horse at odds of 3-1 when the fair odds are slightly over 6-1.

Note that failing to double would also be a major error for White. That would reduce White's average winnings from one pound (if he doubled and Black passed) to £0.70, as Black would win about 14% of the time.

Another example on the same theme:

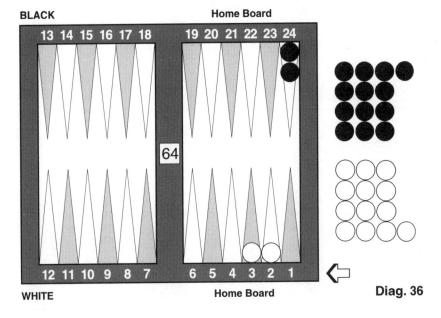

Diag. 36

In case readers get the wrong idea, the cube is usually offered much earlier in the game. However, the odds are easier to understand by looking at simple positions near the end of the game. Here White is on roll. He wins if he can avoid rolling a one. How many rolls contain a one? There are 36 rolls of two dice, and eleven of them contain a one (6-1, 1-6, 5-1, 1-5, 4-1, 1-4, 3-1, 1-3, 2-1, 1-2, 1-1). In case you think 6-1 and 1-6 are the same roll, think of one die being red and the other being blue. You can get a six on the red die and a one on the blue die, or the other way around.

So, on average, White would win 25 times and lose 11 times if the game were played 36 times. This is the last roll and White is favourite, so he should double. As Black is winning more than a quarter of the time, she should accept the cube.

In the positions so far in this chapter, gammons and backgammons were impossible. But a gammon doubles the value of the cube and a backgammon trebles it, though with one proviso:

The Jacoby Rule

In a money game, a gammon or backgammon is only scored as an ordinary win if an initial cube turn has not been made. The purpose of this rule, which does **not** apply in matches, is to prevent too many long games in which a player gets a sudden big advantage in the opening and plays for an undoubled gammon win. It also encourages early cube turns when a player thinks that a gammon win is possible.

Redoubles

Let us return to the position in diagram 34. Black doubles and White decides to accept. The position is now shown with the cube on White's side:

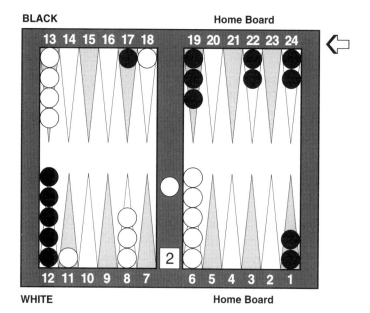

Diag. 37

From this position either side might win a gammon or even a backgammon. If, for example, Black went on to win a gammon and the cube were not turned to a higher level in the remainder of the game, then Black would win four points (2 x 2). The cube is shown on White's side of the board in diagram 37. This means that only he may make the next double (known as a redouble). The opportunity to redouble is available only to the player who has been doubled. We therefore need to modify the 25% rule. In fact, one can generally accept a double with a little less than a 25% chance of winning, as, when you redouble and your opponent passes, you win some games which you would otherwise have lost.

TIP: Because you can redouble, the original 25% rule should really be thought of as a 22% rule

Later in the same game, the following position might arise:

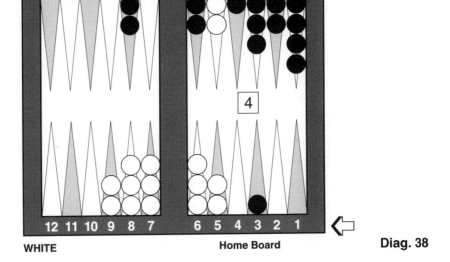

Diag. 38

White has survived the attack and made his 20-point. Then he went on to build blocking points on his side of the board and trapped a black checker. At this juncture he redoubled to four, as shown in diagram 38. Black should decline. She is less than 25% to get her last checker over White's blockade and around to safety. How can we estimate this? Only through experience. There is an acronym which is helpful in making decisions regarding whether to double or accept:

PRAT: Position, Race and Threats

These are the three factors which one should consider when deciding whether to offer or accept a double. Generally a clear advantage in two areas is enough to offer a double. A significant advantage in all three areas is normally a pass. Of course, deciding on the degree of advantage is very important. Take the following position:

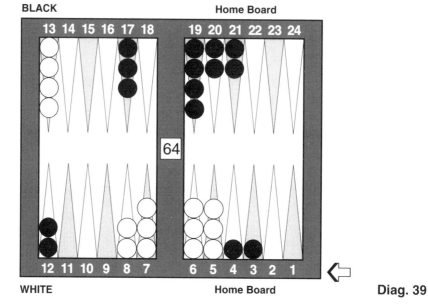

Diag. 39

Position

White has the advantage in position. He has made four blocking points in a row, and has also escaped his two back checkers (they are no longer in Black's home board).

Race

We will learn how to count this exactly in the next chapter. White requires fewer pips to bring his checkers home and bear them off and is therefore ahead in the race.

Threats

White has a number of rolls which make his four- or three-points. These include 5-4, 5-3, 5-2, 4-3, 4-2, 4-1, 3-2, 3-1, 2-1 and various doubles. So White has strong threats.

According to our criteria, therefore, White should double and Black should pass. If we change the position by moving the Black checker on her 22-point to her 21-point, then all of a sudden we eliminate White's threats. The position becomes a high-anchor game, and is a bare double and easy take.

An important factor to estimate when you offer or accept a cube is the percentage of gammons. A doubled gammon scores four points, so even if it only occurs one quarter of the time, that is equivalent to the point that you could have given up. Double early if there is a good chance of winning a gammon.

 WARNING: If you accept a cube, consider the likelihood of being gammoned with a loss of four points

The criteria for accepting a redouble are similar to those for accepting an initial double, but when offering a redouble one should be more conservative. If the cube is on your side, only you can use it. When you redouble you both take away your access to the cube and give access to the opponent.

Too Good

One other category of positions is when you are too good to double or redouble and should play on for the gammon. In the following position White should not redouble, even though Black should pass like a shot if you do.

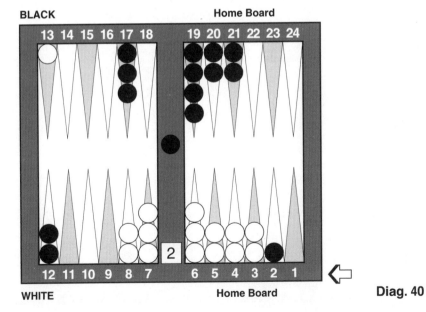

Diag. 40

By playing on you will, on average, win more than the two points you could obtain by doubling now.

Exercise 7: Use PRAT to decide on whether White should double in the following position:

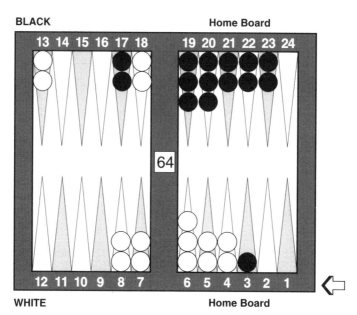

Diag. 41

Exercise 8: Should White redouble here? If doubled, should Black accept?

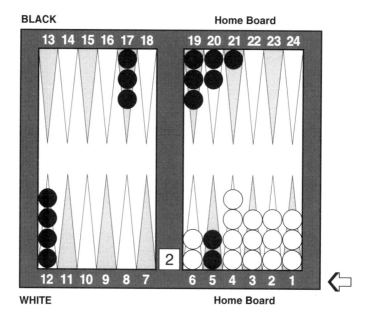

Diag. 42

Chapter Five

The Race

- **How to Count Pips**
- **The 10% Rule**
- **The 12$\frac{1}{2}$% Rule**
- **Crossovers and Wastage**
- **Gaps**
- **Bearing in**

A significant percentage of backgammon games reach a race in which there is only a small amount of skill in moving the checkers. Indeed some players have a 'racing style' in that they attempt to enter a race whenever possible. The skill in a race is in deciding whether to offer or accept a double, and many complex formulae have been devised to assist the player. The gain from their use is limited, and most players will find the rules-of-thumb in this chapter adequate.

How to Count Pips

Most backgammon players are lazy. When you double them in a race they look around the board, maybe noting how many checkers are not yet in the home boards, and take a view on whether to accept. They adopt the same approach to doubling. However, obtaining a good estimate of winning chances in a race requires only simple counting and does not entail learning any tables. Let us take a typical non-contact position (one in which there is no further opportunity to hit a shot):

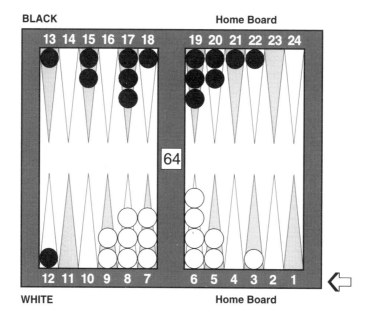

Diag. 43

To evaluate this position we need to establish a pip-count. This is done by totalling the number of pips required by each side to bear off. In White's case the two checkers on the nine-point represent a total of 18 pips, the three on the eight-point a total of 24 pips, and so on. His pip-count is:

$(18+24+21+24+10+3) = 100$

For Black we need to consider the board from her viewpoint, inverting the numbers. Her pip-count is:

$(13+12+20+24+7+18+10+4+3) = 111$

So, we have two separate pip-counts. What next?

The 10% Rule

As a general rule, you should double when you lead by 10% in the pip-count. This means that the difference between the two pip-counts is at least 10% of the leader's pip-count. In our example, the difference in pip-counts is 11 and the leader's pip-count is 100. As a percentage, therefore, the lead is 11%. White should therefore double. To redouble you need a slightly higher lead, about 11%.

The 12$\frac{1}{2}$% Rule

To judge whether to accept any double, we compare the lead with the leader's pip-count. If it is no more than 12$\frac{1}{2}$% (one eighth), then you should accept. More and you should pass. In our example the lead is 11%, so Black should accept.

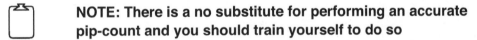

NOTE: There is a no substitute for performing an accurate pip-count and you should train yourself to do so

Other books have quoted slightly different figures to the above, but the author is fortunate to be writing this book in the age of very strong backgammon computers, which can play races almost perfectly. They have shown that there has been a tendency among most players to double prematurely in races. Indeed if the Black checker on her 13-point were moved to her 11-point, then the lead would be 9 pips, or 9%. The position would not quite be a double.

Crossovers and Wastage

The above two rules are good general guidelines for judging races, but a couple of worthwhile refinements can be added. Before a player can begin bearing off, he must get all his checkers into the home board. The player with more checkers outside the home board is therefore at a disadvantage, as he is likely to start bearing off later. The board comprises four quadrants of six points each and the move of a checker from one quadrant of the board into another is known as a crossover. Take the following position:

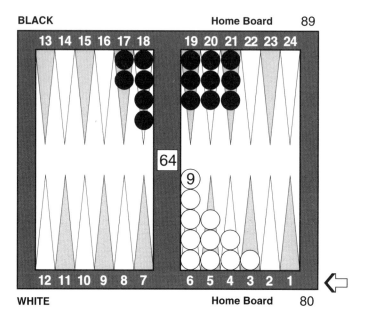

White is on roll and the pip-count of White: 80 Black: 89 is shown at the top and bottom of the board. This represents a lead of 9 which is more than 10% of 80 but less than 12^1/$_2$%. Black has six checkers outside her board, and this is to her disadvantage. However, these extra crossovers are much less important than some previous authors have claimed. To Black's pip-count we should add about half a pip for each extra crossover. So we add three to Black's pip-count, which increases it to 92. White's position is not perfect either. With nine checkers on the six-point, White will end up moving checkers from the six-point to a lower point, unless he rolls a lot of sixes. Having too many checkers on any point requires an adjustment. When you have them all on the ace-point or deuce-point you will bear off every roll. However, your pip-count still needs adjusting to reflect the wastage when you roll high numbers and bear off checkers from the low points.

To any pip-count we should add:

a) two pips for each checker over two on the one-point.

b) one pip for each checker over two on the two-point.

c) half a pip for each checker in excess of five on any point

So in our example we penalise White two pips for the four surplus checkers on the six-point. This makes White's pip-count 82. So the adjusted pip-count is 82-92, a lead of ten. This is a lead between 10% and 12½%, so White should double and Black should take.

Gaps

One other distributional feature which can affect the pip-count is the gap. If, in the bear-off, you have a point in your home board not occupied by any checkers then this is a disadvantage. Take the following position:

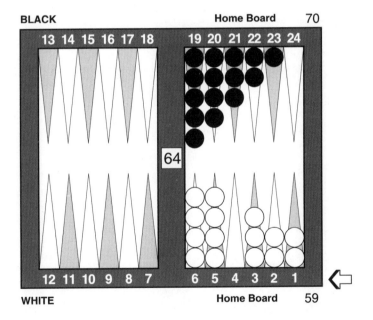

Diag. 45

Black has an optimal distribution, sometimes referred to as the 'Golden Triangle'. White, on the other hand, has a gap on his four-point. This means that any fours will need to be played from the five- or six-points. To adjust a pip-count for gaps, we would ideally wish to take into account the number of checkers above the gap, and the remaining distribution.

However, a rough-and-ready rule is as follows:

a) for a gap on the four-point, add four to the pip-count.

b) for a gap on the five-point, add three to the pip-count.

c) for a gap on the three-point, add two to the pip-count.

d) for a gap on the two-point, add one to the pip-count.

The above assumes that you have at least six checkers on points above the gap, and is a good approximation. In our example, we therefore add four to White's pip-count, giving an adjusted count of 63-70. The lead is seven, which is between 10% and 12$^{1}/_{2}$% of 63. Therefore White should double and Black should take. This is confirmed by the database of US endgame authority Hugh Sconyers.

Bearing in

 TIP: Since it is to your disadvantage to have a gap, when you are moving your remaining checkers into the home board, you should aim to fill any gaps if possible

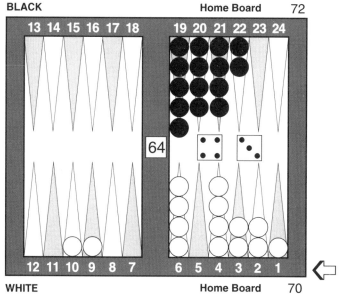

Diag. 46

White has rolled a 4-3 in the above position and can make two crossovers with 10/6 9/6. However, this is quite a large mistake, as avoiding a gap is more important than making a crossover. The correct play is to fill the gap with 9/5 10/7.

Exercise 9: Count the following race.
a) Should White double? b) Should Black accept?

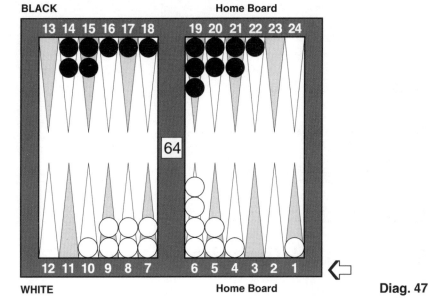

Diag. 47

Exercise 10: You are given the pip count this time.
Use the rules for adjustment in this chapter to decide
a) Should White double? b) Should Black accept?

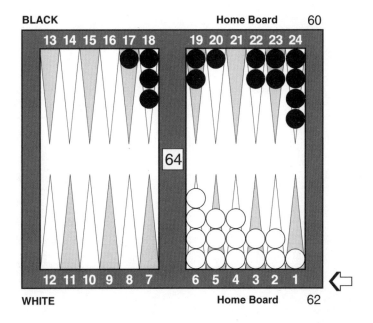

Diag. 48

Chapter Six

The Bear-Off

- **Standard Positions**
- **General Rules**
- **Checker Plays**
- **Unusual Techniques**

An exact calculation of every position with all fifteen checkers in each home board has been conducted by the American expert Hugh Sconyers. The full database can be accessed only by subscribers to the Internet server GamesGrid, but the most useful parts of the database are available on CD-Rom from the suppliers on page 117. The occasions on which one needs to access this database are rare and most players will find that a few basic rules suffice.

Standard Positions

There is rarely a difficult problem with moving the checkers in the bear-off. However, decisions on whether to double or take are frequent. Indeed, the decision may sometimes be different when the cube is in the centre (not yet turned) and when it is owned by the player. We start with a position which everyone needs to know:

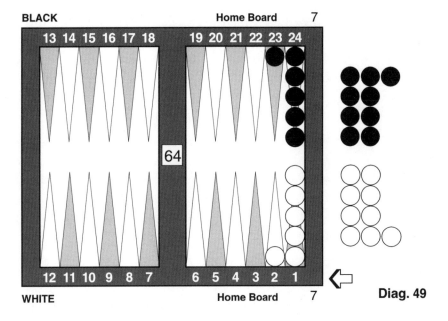

Diag. 49

In this position each side is guaranteed to remove all six checkers in no more than three rolls. It is therefore known as a three-roll position. An exact calculation shows that White wins almost 79% of the time. White should double and Black should pass. If the cube were owned by White, he would also redouble and again Black would pass.

Diagram 49 falls into the category of what we call 'no-miss' positions, where each player is guaranteed to bear off at least two checkers each turn. The following are the correct cube actions for the various no-miss positions:

Two Rolls v Two Rolls	**Double, Redouble, Pass**
Three Rolls v Three Rolls	**Double, Redouble, Pass**
Four Rolls v Four Rolls	**Double, Redouble, Take**
Five+ Rolls v Five+ Rolls	**Double, no Redouble, Take**

The above are only applicable where both sides require the same number of rolls, assuming neither gets a double.

NOTE: All positions where the person on roll requires one fewer roll to bear off than the opponent are doubles, redoubles and passes. Where the person on roll requires one more roll to bear off than the opponent, then that player should neither double nor redouble.

You will see above that when both sides require five or more rolls, then the position is an initial double, but not a redouble. This is because redoubling transfers access to the cube to your opponent. You do better holding off until you are nearer the winning post, so that you get to play the game until the end if your opponent rolls a double before you.

Diagram 49 would have the same analysis if all six checkers of each side were on the ace-point. However, if some checkers were on higher points, so that either side had immediate or later 'missing' rolls (rolls which do not bear off two checkers), then the position would not necessarily conform to the chart given above.

General Rules

In the majority of endgames, neither player has a pure no-miss position. It is more likely that he has several checkers on higher points. The race rules from the last chapter are not at all accurate for pip counts below 20, and are unreliable between 20 and 50. Therefore we present some general rules here, which should be adequate for most positions. The keen student may want to consult more specialist works for all one- and two-checker positions.

a) If the player on roll has only one remaining home-board checker then the position is a double, redouble and pass. There are a few positions in which the pass is borderline, but passing is still as correct as taking.

b) A player on roll with two checkers should double or redouble if he is a favourite to bear off in one roll.

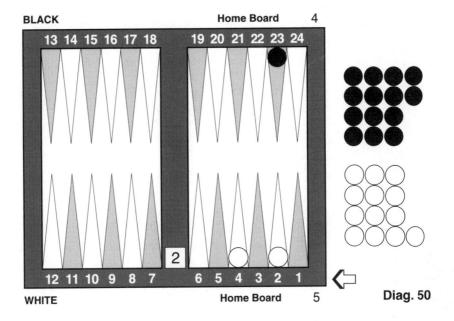

Diag. 50

Here White has 23 numbers which win and 13 which lose (all ones plus 3-2). White should redouble. As White misses more than 25% of the time, Black should accept.

There are a few exceptions to our rule b) in that there are a handful of positions which are doubles but not redoubles. However the error in redoubling them is very slight.

c) With two checkers each, or with two checkers against one, when the player on roll does not have 27 or more winning rolls, you should accept a double if the pip count is at least equal, otherwise decline. A player can usually double when trailing by up to two pips, but no more.

This is a good general rule, but again there are a few exceptions and the player following it may make a small error. For example, with two checkers each on the three-point, four-point or five-point, it is slightly better to pass.

d) With two checkers for the player on roll against three checkers it is almost always a pass. The exceptions occur when the two checkers are on the six-point.

e) With three checkers for the player on roll against two, you should not double if your opponent is favourite to get off next turn. Again there are one or two exceptions. Otherwise you can double when you are trailing by up to two pips. If your pip-count is more than 12, it is usually wrong to double. If the player not on roll trails in the pip-count, and has a pip-count of nine or more, then it is usually a pass.

f) With three checkers each, if the player on roll has ten or fewer pips it is nearly always a double, or redouble, and pass. With a pip-count of 11 or 12 it is nearly always a double, and the opponent usually needs the same pip-count to take. With pip-counts of 13 or more, you can double with a pip-count that is the same as the opponent's. She should take with a pip-count of one more than you.

The above may seem a bit complicated, but it is not imperative that these rules are learnt verbatim. Most bear-off cube decisions can be judged by the experienced player. Let us examine a position and see if it conforms with our rules:

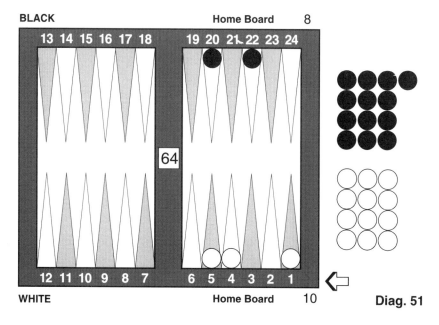

Diag. 51

An exact calculation shows that this position is a correct double and a take (if White owned the cube it would be a correct redouble too). The opponent is not favourite to get off next turn, and White trails by no more than two pips, so, according to our rule (e), White should double and Black should take.

Checker Plays

It is rare that there is a crucial checker play in the bear-off, provided the player follows these simple rules:

a) Always bear off a checker if you can.

b) If you cannot bear off a checker, then fill the highest available gap, but not by creating a new gap.

c) If you cannot bear-off a checker, nor fill a gap, then move from the point with the most checkers.

WARNING: A gap when bearing off can cause you to miss. Look to see whether you can avoid one

These rules are more than adequate to cover 99% of endgames. Let us see how we would apply them to the following position:

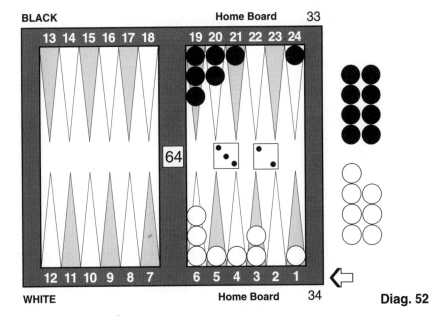

Diag. 52

With the three, White can bear off, so he should. With the two, he can fill a gap with 4/2, but this creates a new gap, so he should play off the heaviest point with 6/4.

Unusual Techniques

Sometimes it is necessary to play for doubles in the bear-off, and the above rules go out of the window. If you are a huge underdog, then you need to maximise the number of doubles which will help you win. Take the following position:

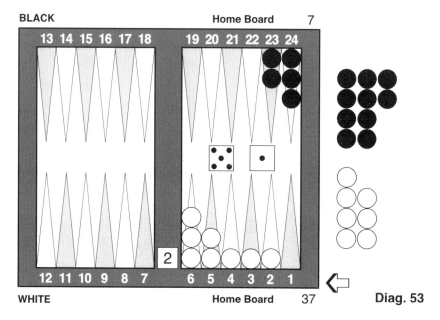

Diag. 53

Black is certain to be off in three rolls, so that White needs to get off in two rolls after this one, while hoping that his opponent does not get a double. It is clear that White is a big underdog, and needs to start thinking 'doubles". After bearing off a checker with the five, White must play an ace. An inspection shows that White must roll a 6-6 on one of the next two rolls to have any chance. This will bear off the four remaining checkers on the six- and five-points. The right ace is therefore the peculiar 3/2, allowing 2-2 to bear off the remaining checkers on the other roll. This is from an actual game in which the author was White, found the correct play, and rolled 6-6, 2-2 ...

One other important consideration in the bear-off is to maintain as smooth a distribution as possible.

 WARNING: Avoid situations where certain numbers have to be played by stacking an extra checker on a point with four or five checkers already.

Occasionally it is necessary to look for an opportunity to avoid a gap, even wasting a pip or two:

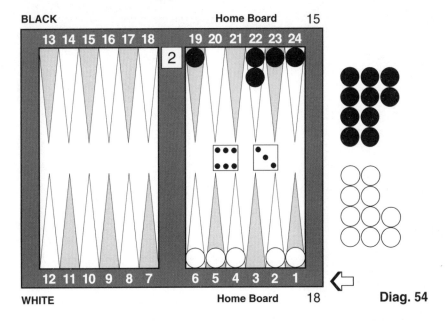

Diag. 54

Here the correct play is to play the smaller number first with 6/3 and then to bear off with 5/o. If you play the six first, then either 4/1 or 5/2 leaves a gap. However, in the next example, you should play 6/o 4/1. You then have five checkers left, so can afford one roll in which you bear off only one checker.

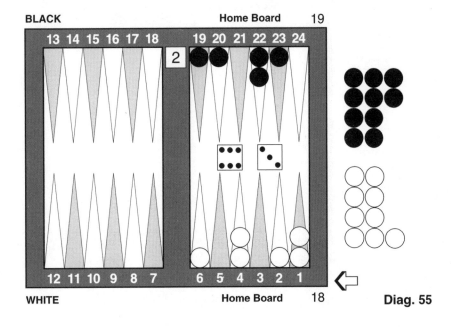

Diag. 55

Exercise 11: Should White double? Should Black take?

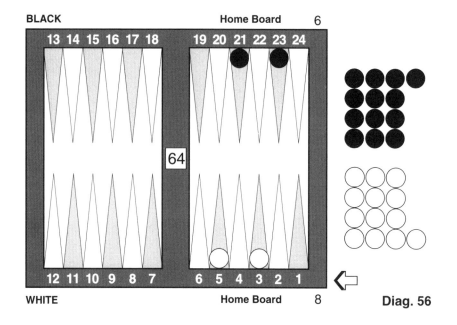

Diag. 56

Exercise 12: White is to play a 4-3 in the next position. How would you play?

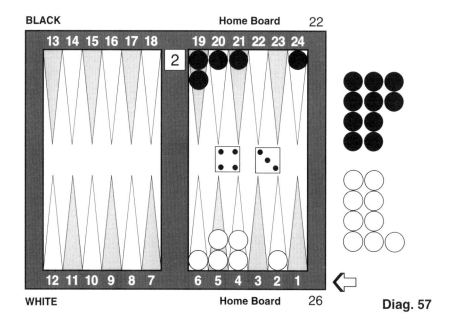

Diag. 57

Chapter Seven

Priming Games

- **Important Features**
- **Golden Rules**
- **Changing Plans**

Important Features

As we stated in the chapter on basic strategy, the object of the opening stage is to build blocking points which impede the movement of the opposing checkers. Sometimes this is ineffective and the opponent escapes his back checkers before a blockade is established. Often, however, the back checkers remain trapped and an interesting struggle called a priming game results. Take the following position:

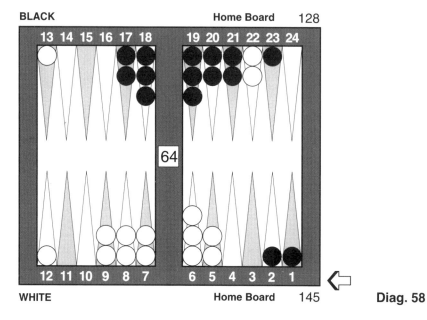

Diag. 58

Both sides have made a five-prime, a blockade of five points in a row. To the untutored eye the position may look level. How do we assess positions in which there are checkers trapped behind a prime? The following factors are important:

a) The length of the prime. A six-prime is much stronger than a five-prime and the latter is much stronger than a four-prime, etc. This is the single most important factor.

b) Where the trapped checkers are. In diagram 58, White's checkers are at the edge of the prime, so that they can jump over it with any six. Black's checkers are not.

c) Timing. This is a measure of the number of spare pips which can be played before one is forced to give up one of the points in the prime. To calculate your timing and your opponent's, assume that you will not be able to move the trapped checkers. So in diagram 58, White has 28 spare pips (12 with the checker on the 13-point, 11 with the checker on the 12-point and five with the checker on the six-point) before he is forced to give up one of the points in the six-prime. Black has 17 spare pips (12 on her side of the board, and five on White's side). Of course, either player may jump over the prime, creating many extra pips of timing, and this must be borne in mind.

d) Which side has an anchor. Usually it is better to have an anchor, as this stops the opponent adopting an alternative plan of attacking. It is also insurance against the back checkers being closed out with a possible gammon loss.

e) The race is not the main concern in a priming battle. It will play a part only if the character of the position changes.

In our example opposite, White has all the advantages, and many intermediate players would double here.

 TIP: However, the basic rule in a priming game is to wait to escape one checker, or for your opponent's prime to reduce to fewer than five points, before you double

White should not double, and Black has an easy take.

In diagram 59, Black's blockade has been reduced to a four-prime. White should now double and Black should pass.

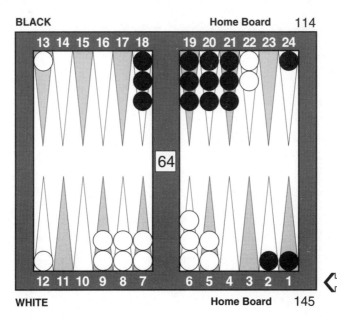

Diag. 59

Golden Rules

What are the golden rules for playing priming games? The richness of the play does not allow us to set hard and fast rules, and there will be many exceptions. However, the following guidelines may be useful.

a) Hitting opposing checkers to get them behind your prime is usually a good idea. The exceptions occur when you do not want the opponent to stay on the bar.

The following position is an instructive example:

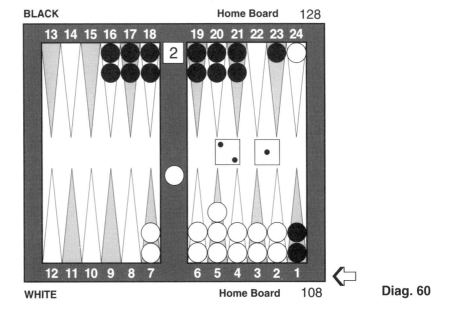

Diag. 60

Black has just made the good play of hitting on her two-point and there is a temptation to hit back with the 2-1. This should be resisted. White should play b/24 24/22. Whatever Black rolls next will break her six-prime. The problem with hitting is that Black may stay on the bar for several rolls, and White may soon be forced to break his own six-prime.

b) Getting to the edge of the opposing prime is beneficial, even if it is a six-prime. In our above example, after entering without hitting, it is much better to move up with 24/22 than to play passively with 5/3. As soon as Black's prime breaks, you will be poised to jump over it.

c) Usually jump over the prime if you can. This may apply even though there is something else attractive to play. For example:

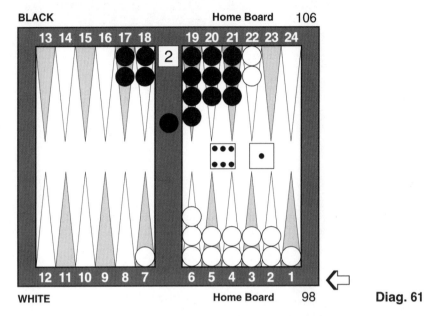

BLACK   Home Board   106

13 14 15 16 17 18   19 20 21 22 23 24

12 11 10 9 8 7   6 5 4 3 2 1

WHITE   Home Board   98   Diag. 61

Here the correct six is 22/16 and the ace is not of great importance (16/15 is best). Another useful backgammon proverb is 'Sixes don't grow on trees'.

TIP: The importance of jumping the prime cannot be overemphasised and is often right even though you seem to have plenty of time

d) Usually hit an opponent's checker which is at the edge of your prime: You should often take quite large risks to prevent your opponent jumping away to safety. If you hit her, she has to hit back and jump (two tasks); if you leave her there she just has to jump (one task).

e) Extend your prime if you can. The earlier examples in diagrams 58 and 59 showed the difference between a five-prime and a four-prime. Lengthening your prime usually takes priority over any other strategy.

f) Sometimes give up trying to win the game and settle for avoiding a gammon loss. Priming games have a habit of collapsing at times, and a position can disintegrate to the point where trying to win takes too many risks and the most likely result is that you get gammoned:

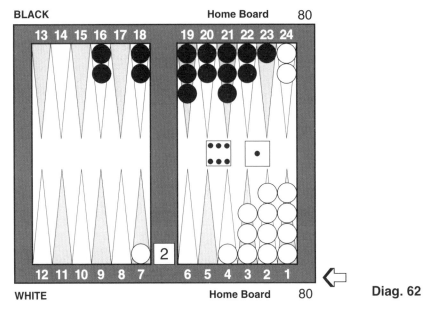

BLACK   Home Board   80

WHITE   Home Board   80   Diag. 62

Here the best play to win the game is to hit and jump out. It follows all the earlier advice. Unfortunately there is a big downside. If Black hits any of the four loose White checkers, she has an excellent chance of sweeping them up and going on to win a gammon. Prudence dictates **not** hitting here and simply sitting tight with 7/1 4/3. White is unlikely to get a third checker sent back now, and the most likely result is a single (non-gammon) win for Black. Another backgammon proverb: 'Second place is no disgrace'.

There are situations where gammons are irrelevant however. A section of Chapter Twelve discusses the differences between match play and money play. If you are playing a one-point match, then the sole object is to win the game, and gammons do not count extra. If you are playing a five-point match and the score is 4-4, the same applies. This situation is known as 'double match point'. In such cases you would hit in diagram 62, and jump out, with a slight chance (about 10%) of getting lucky and winning.

g) One other tip when playing a priming game is that if you have a six-prime and your opponent doesn't, then split your back checkers. If he attacks, you will be quite happy to spend time on the bar. If he doesn't you will have greater flexibility with the back checkers split.

Changing Plans

Even though you start out playing a priming game, it is important to be prepared to change plans. Ideally, you will escape your back checkers and continue to contain your opponent's back checkers as her prime crumbles. But life is never as simple as that. You need to look out for the opportunity to change tack when things do not go according to plan. A large double can destroy your timing, so that you no longer have spare pips to play. Take this position:

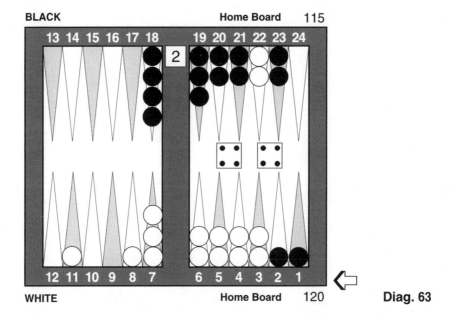

Diag. 63

White had been progressing nicely with the longer prime, but has now rolled a large double. Many players would be pleased that they can just about keep their five-prime intact and play 11/3 7/3 8/4. However, this is the time to change tack, and play the seemingly anti-positional 6/2*(2) 5/1*(2)! Black then has two checkers on the bar, and this should give White time to escape the two checkers on the 22-point.

Another possibility to change tack in a priming game is when you jump over the opponent's prime, but she has many builders in position. You should hit a checker on your side of the board at the same time as a 'tempo play', taking away half your opponent's roll. She then has to use one number to enter, making it harder for her to attack on the other side.

Exercise 13: How should White play 3-2 in the following position?

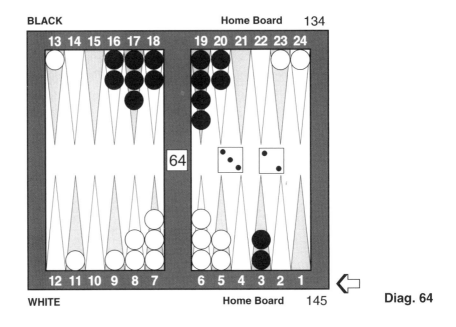

Diag. 64

Exercise 14: Should White double? Should Black take?

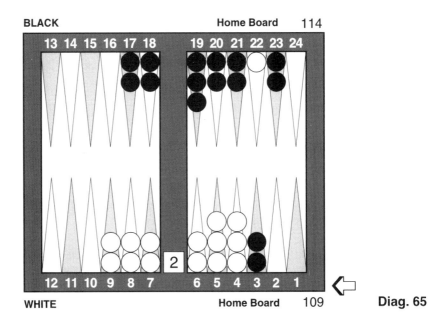

Diag. 65

Chapter Eight

The Blitz

- **A Typical Blitz**
- **When to Double**
- **The Failed Blitz**

A blitz is defined in the Glossary of this book as 'an attack on one or more of your opponent's back checkers with the aim of repeatedly sending them to the bar.' The ultimate purpose of a blitz is to close out one or more checkers, by making all six points in your home board.

Of course, the opponent will not willingly co-operate in this plan, and your blitz may fail the moment an opponent makes an anchor — any point in your board. Most blitzes start when you hit an opposing checker in your own board and the opponent fails to hit back.

A Typical Blitz

Let us return to diagram 7 on page 14, and continue a possible game:

1	4-3:	**24/20 13/10**	6-3:	**24/15***
2	6-1:	**b/18**	3-3:	**13/7* 8/5(2)***

White now gets a 4-3 and enters with both checkers:

3	4-3:	**b/21 b/22**

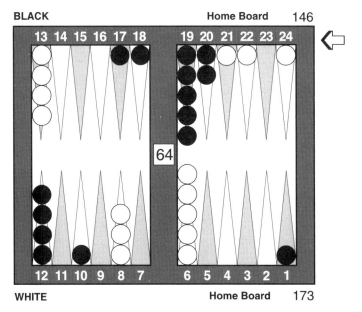

Diag. 66

This is a good roll, but Black still offers a double. She is intending to play a blitz and to use the builders on her seven-point and eight-point to attack the white blots in her board.

This looks very worrying for White and many beginners would turn down the double. However, although it is a correct double, it is also right for White to accept.

TIP: If you do not have a checker on the bar, and the opponent has only a two-point board at present, then you should usually accept a cube. If she has a three-point board, and many builders in position, then you should probably drop

Black doubles and White accepts

3   ...   4-1:   8/4* 4/3*

Black does not roll a number which allows her to make another inner-board point, but she is able to hit two checkers. It is vital to keep the initiative in a blitz. Let us see the new position:

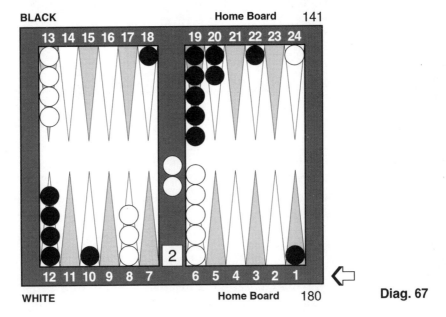

Diag. 67

The cube is now on White's side of the board, on 2, and Black is attacking vigorously. The priorities for the player of a blitz are:

a) to make new inner-board points.

b) to put further checkers on the bar.

c) to bring down extra builders into attacking positions.

The person being blitzed has but one aim, and that is largely outside his control: to make an anchor, and not to give it up! White would like to get a one to anchor on his 24-point. Hitting any blot in Black's board will also help.

4	6-4:	b/21

White gets one checker in and Black gets a good reply which allows her to continue the attack: **2-2**. How should she play?

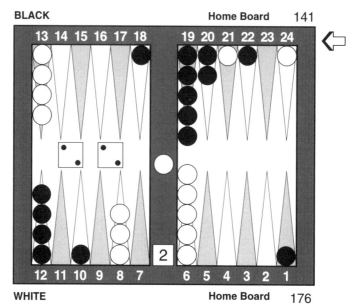

Black to play 2-2   Diag. 68

The correct way to play is to make the four-point with two checkers from the six-point and to cover the checker on the three-point from the bar-point. Making a new inner-board point takes priority over hitting another checker with 3/1*.

4	...		2-2:	6/4*(2) 7/3
5	6-5:	**No entry**		

White compounds his problems by not entering. From here Black will hit whenever she can in her home board, but not by giving up an existing point to do so. If Black can make all six points in her board, White will be almost certain to lose a gammon. In that case Black will score four points, as the cube has already been turned to two.

6	...		6-5:	13/7 6/1*

As we explained earlier, White's plan is to make an anchor, and therefore Black should hit on the one-point to forestall this plan. A blitz should never be played half-heartedly.

6	5-3:	**No entry**	6/4:	7/1 13/9

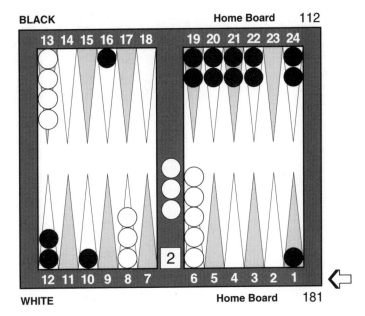

BLACK   Home Board   112

WHITE   Home Board   181   **Diag. 69**

Black has made further progress and White is in deep trouble. Black will bring more builders down from the mid-point and as soon as White enters on his 23-point, she will use one of these to hit White, not worrying about being hit back. Probably Black will close White out and win a gammon, though there is no such thing as a certainty, and sometimes White will turn round such a game and win.

When to Double

The time to make an initial double in a blitz is usually when the opponent fails to enter with one of his checkers and you have already made two, or preferably three, home-board points. In our example above, Black had only made two points, but she had several checkers poised in attacking positions.

NOTE: Remember that you cannot win a gammon in a money game if you have not doubled — the Jacoby Rule. If the position can change quickly, get your double in early.

If you have an anchor the position is usually a take. A crucial factor is the number of builders which are suitably placed for making new points. If there are no builders in position, then even with three points made, a double may be premature. In the following position, even though White failed to enter on his previous turn, a double would still be incorrect:

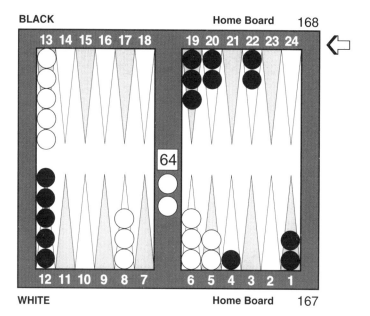

Diag. 70

 WARNING: You should wait until you have some threats before doubling. Think back to our doubling acronym PRAT. The race is equal and Black is threatening little. So, no double

However, if Black has several builders poised, it may be a pass even though there are no checkers on the bar. In the next position White has a clear pass:

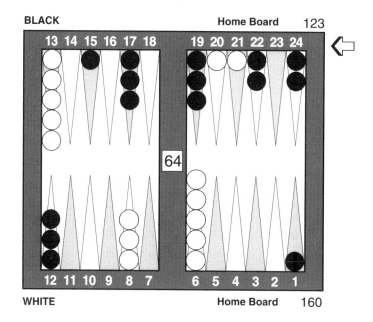

Diag. 71

It is hard to work out whether to double in a blitz position, and whether the position is a take. You should therefore double if you are unsure, as your opponent will face a tough decision. American expert Kit Woolsey devised a rule for doubling:

TIP: If you do not know yourself if the position is a take, then you should double

The race is less of a factor in a blitz, as a player often starts a blitz with a double which gains in the race. However, the moment the opponent makes an anchor, the position can change rapidly as explained in the next section.

The Failed Blitz

A failed blitz occurs when the opponent anchors. It may well be that the position is still good, because the opponent made an anchor only very late in the game. However, when the opponent anchors at the start of a blitz, the position can rapidly turn sour. In the following example, Black began with an early 5-5, but White has just rolled 4-4, entering both checkers while hitting and Black has failed to enter in reply.

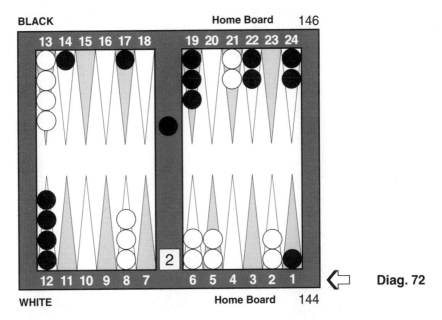

Diag. 72

Now White has a powerful redouble and Black should pass. The checkers on Black's three-point and ace-point are out of play, and White is threatening to hit more checkers.

Exercise 15: Should White double? Should Black take?

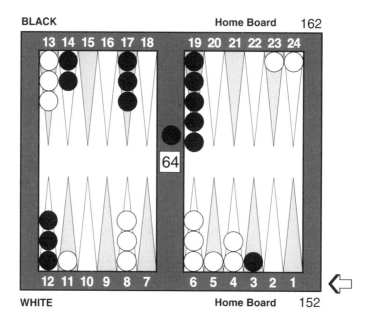

Diag. 73

Exercise 16: White has a choice of several reasonable moves with a 6-3. Which is best?

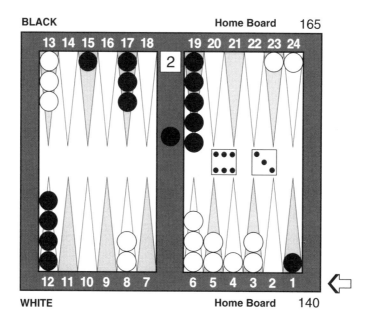

Diag. 74

Chapter Nine

Holding Games

- **What is a Holding Game?**
- **Mid-Point v Anchor**
- **Mid-Point v Bar-Point**
- **High Anchors**
- **Low Anchors**
- **Multiple Anchors**

What is a Holding Game?

Any position in which both sides have one or two anchors or outfield points in the opposing half of the board and their remaining checkers on their own side of the board is classed as a holding game. If the anchor is behind a prime of four or more checkers, then the position is essentially a priming game. In a holding game, the checkers on the anchor or outfield point are usually able to advance each turn, but at the cost of leaving one or more direct shots. For example:

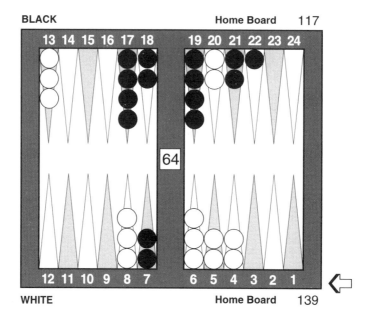

Diag. 75

This is a typical mutual holding game. White has an anchor and an outfield point on the opponent's side of the board, and Black has an anchor on White's side. Black is leading in the race, but she has a problem bringing her checkers on White's bar-point to safety. White is playing a waiting game. He may move both checkers from his 20-point at some stage, but his main way of winning the game is to hit one of Black's two checkers currently on White's bar-point when they later move. Typical plans in a holding game are:

a) To move an anchor with a double. Black's best rolls next turn are 5-5, 4-4, 3-3 and 2-2 in that order. She would use them to move the two checkers on her 18-point.

b) To hit a shot. This is a higher priority for White, but Black would also hit a shot, if she can also cover her blot. Hitting a shot is one of the safest ways to clear an anchor.

c) To preserve spare sixes. As soon as Black has cleared her seven-point and eight-point in diagram 75, she will have to play her next six from her 18-point, moving the smaller number first. She won't be allowed to play the smaller number elsewhere and say, 'I have no six.' Black should therefore delay clearing her seven- and eight-points until she has resolved the problem with her back two checkers.

d) Keep as strong a board as possible. As either side is keen to hit a checker, a strong board is clearly an advantage. If White had two or three blots in an untidy board, Black could take the opportunity to run off her anchor, as being hit would give her return shots from the bar.

Mid-Point v Anchor

The simplest holding game is one of a single outfield point against a single anchor. Usually, but not necessarily, the outfield point is the mid-point. The two points may be any number of pips apart, with a minimum number of three. A common type of position is the following in which the points are eight pips apart.

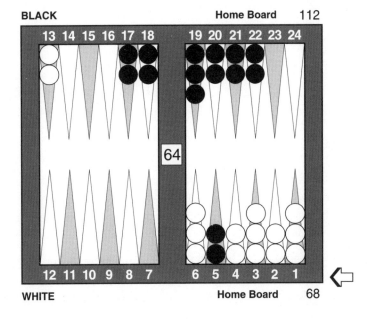

Diag. 76

The doubling strategy in holding games is fairly clearly defined. The positions are not that complicated and are handled well by computers, which can play a large number of sample games from any position. The first point to make is that it is much better for the player trailing in the race if the outfield point and anchor (or even two outfield points) are six or fewer pips apart. The reason for this is that if the race leader is forced to move off the outfield point, then the other player gets a direct shot of six or fewer pips.

 TIP: Most positions with the two points seven, eight or nine pips apart are also easy takes for the person way behind in the race

Take our position in diagram 76. Black has many ways she can win:

a) After White moves one checker off the mid-point, she rolls an eight. The chances of rolling an eight each turn are exactly one in six (17%).

b) White may roll a 6-2 and be forced to leave a direct shot.

c) White may come in safely, say with a 4-3, played 13/6, but then be unable to bring his final checker to safety next turn.

d) White may bring both checkers to safety, but then Black may get a last-ditch shot when White is forced to leave a blot on his six-point, and Black hits it.

e) White may come home safely, but Black wins the race with a flurry of high doubles.

So we can see that Black has many ways to win. Indeed Black wins a total of around 30% of games from this position and it is correct for White to double and for Black to take.

Mid-Point v Bar-Point

It will come as no surprise that as the race trailer can take a double when the outfield point and anchor are seven to nine pips apart, he can also usually take when the two points are six or fewer pips apart.

Indeed, in positions where the outfield point and anchor are five or six pips apart, it is incorrect to double. The right strategy is to wait until your outfield point is half-cleared and then to double. We can change diagram 76 slightly to illustrate this:

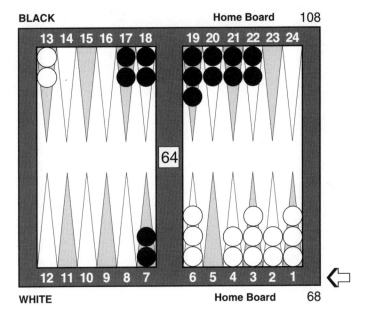

Diag. 77

Black's anchor has been shifted to White's bar-point, and this increases her winning chances considerably. Unless White rolls a double, he will soon leave a direct six-shot when he is forced to move one man from his mid-point, and Black will be nearly 50-50 to hit this. Black does not always get a shot, but her overall winning chances are around 40% and it is premature for White to double.

We can make further changes to the above position to reduce the gap between the anchor and outfield point. If the two black checkers on her 18-point are moved to her 17-point or 16-point, then White has a correct double and Black a correct take. Moving them to her 15-point makes the position a pass. White can then roll 6-5, 6-4 and 5-4, or most doubles, to break contact and win the race easily.

High Anchors

Another common type of position is when one side has an anchor on his 21-point or 20-point and the opponent has two or three points made in front of the anchor. These differ from outfield point v anchor positions in that the race leader has some landing points for his remaining checkers. Frequently both players still have their mid-points, as in this position:

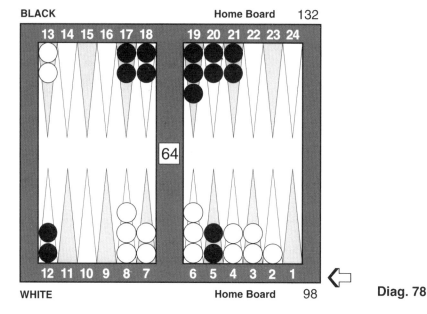

Diag. 78

The evaluation of high-anchor positions depends on a number of factors:

a) The race. A position is never a double if it would not be a double without contact. The player with the anchor can usually take with a race deficit of 20%, often more.

b) Which anchor you have. The 20-point is much better than the 21-point, and low anchors are weaker, but offer more chances than previous authors have claimed.

c) Whether the mid-point still has to be cleared. If it does, then this makes it more likely that the player with a high-anchor can take.

d) The number of points made in front of the anchor. If there are three landing points for the checkers on the mid-point, this tends to make the position a pass, and the above position is indeed a double for White and a narrow pass for Black. However, move the three men on White's eight-point to his six-point and it is a take.

e) Whether there are gaps in front of the anchor. If the two checkers on White's bar-point were moved to the nine-point or ten-point, then it would be a take for Black.

Low Anchors

Some authors have claimed that if you have a pass according to the rules for accepting a cube in a race, then you should pass with a low anchor. However, this over-simplifies the issue, and a number of other factors need to be taken into account:

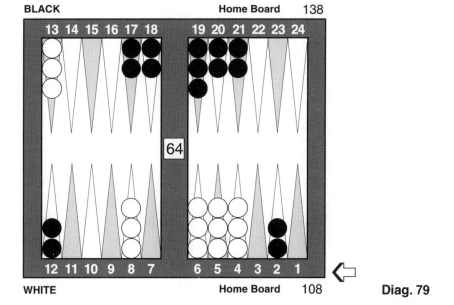

Diag. 79

Here Black has the two-anchor, but is 30 pips behind in the race. White has a strong double, but Black still has a correct take. The factors which influence this decision are as follows:

a) The race, as ever, is of importance. Black's chances in the race (here about 12%) should be added to her main way of winning, which is hitting a shot as White bears in.

b) Which anchor Black has. The ace-point is the worst of the three low anchors. The two-point and three-point are about the same. The advantage of the former is that it is more difficult for White to play safely behind the anchor, as only the ace-point is available for this purpose.

c) Whether White has made both the seven-point and five-point. Here the seven-point is still open, which makes it harder for White to bring his remaining checkers in safely. Move two of White's spare checkers from his home board back to the seven-point and Black has to pass.

d) Whether Black still has her mid-point. Moving Black's two checkers from her mid-point to her 11-point would make the position a pass.

e) Whether White has checkers buried on the ace-point. If White's spares on his six-point and five-point were moved to his ace-point, it would be premature for White to double.

Multiple Anchors

Positions with two high anchors have similarities with what are termed backgames, the subject of the next chapter, in which the player with the anchors must hit a shot to have any chance of winning. For example:

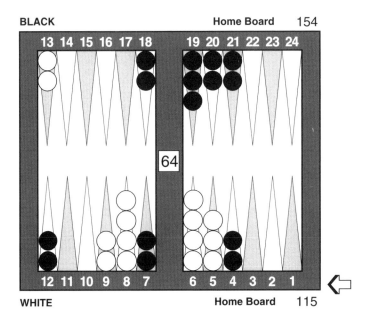

Diag. 80

If White clears the mid-point safely, Black will have a big pass, so White should double now.

WARNING: It is easy to overrate the value of two anchors one of which is the opponent's bar-point.

Black's position will usually transpose into one of the single-anchor positions discussed earlier in this chapter, or she may keep both her anchors if White goes further ahead in the race. Black is winning around 25% of the time and has a narrow take, according to roll-outs by the computer program Snowie 3.

Exercise 17: Should White double? Should Black take?

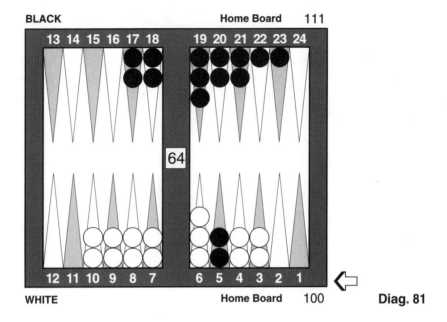

Diag. 81

Exercise 18: White to play a 2-2

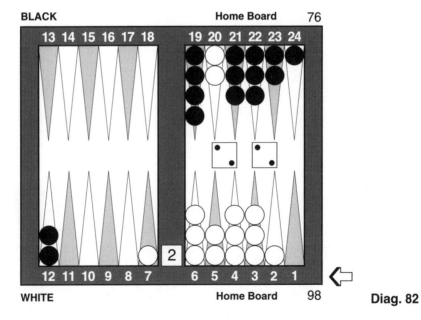

Diag. 82

Chapter Ten

Backgames

- **What is a Backgame?**
- **Doubling Strategy**
- **Different anchors**
- **'Super-Backgames'**

What is a Backgame?

A backgame is a position in which you hold two or more anchors in the opponent's board and the opponent has made several points in front of these checkers. Usually he has also escaped his rear checkers and is ahead in the race. Your main winning strategy is to hit a checker late in the game and then contain it. This is an example of a typical backgame:

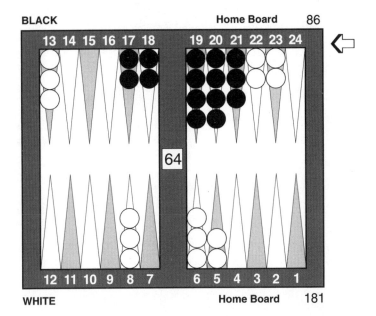

Diag. 83

As you can see, White is almost 100 pips down in the race, so he will have to hit a shot to win. In addition, he will need to contain the hit checker, then bring his other checkers around the board, and finally form a six-prime. The above position is an example of a backgame in which White has all the ingredients necessary to have a playable position. Indeed for Black to double here would be premature and White would have an easy take. What is the strategy for each player?

White
He will keep the anchors on the 22- and 23-points and aim to make new points on the other side. The priority is to make his bar-point and four-point quickly, and then to wait for a shot. After he makes a closed board on his side, he will come off the 22-point in preference to breaking his board.

Black

Her main aim is to avoid leaving a shot! Of course, that is largely outside her control. She leaves a shot immediately, for example, with 6-4 or 6-5. If she has a choice, she will clear points from the back (a general rule). Thus, in diagram 83, Black should clear the eight-point first, then the seven-point. Thereafter she will aim to maintain a smooth distribution and clear points whenever possible.

TIP: 'A point cleared is a point not to be feared,' states yet another backgammon proverb

What are the important features of a backgame?

Timing

The person playing the backgame must have good timing.

NOTE: Timing is a count of the number of pips you can play before you have to move off an anchor or break your board

Once your opponent has her first opportunity to blot you need to still have 20-25 spare pips. In diagram 83, White has 54 pips to play before he has to break his board. He has excellent timing. Let us change the position so that White has a stronger board, but worse timing:

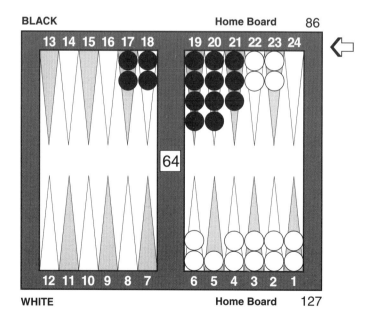

Diag. 84

We have moved White forward by those 54 pips, so that he is

forced either to break his board or run from an anchor next turn. Now the position is a big pass for White.

Which Anchors?

As we shall see later, which two anchors you own makes a big difference to your winning chances. Generally it pays to have the opponent's three-point, plus one other point.

Distribution

It is important for both players to have their checkers in play. If Black's spares on her three home-board points were all on the ace-point in diagram 83, we would have this position:

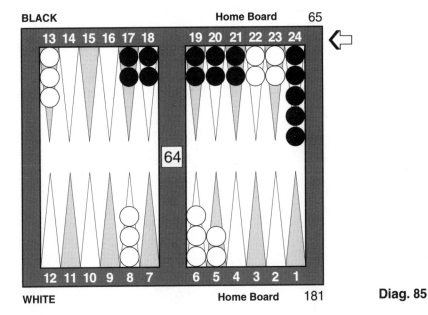

Diag. 85

Now, not only is it wrong for Black to double, but, in a game played for money, White should beaver (if this rule is being played) .This means that he turns the cube to 4, but keeps it on his side of the board. A double which gets beavered usually shows a large misjudgment by one player!

Gaps

So far we have looked at positions in which the opponent of the person playing the backgame has an unbroken prime in front of the two anchors. If that person has a gap in the prime, then the winning chances of the backgame player go up considerably. Moving the checkers from Black's seven-point to her nine-point in diagram 83 increases White's winning chances significantly.

Doubling Strategy

From our comments on whether players should double previous positions, the astute reader may have guessed a rule for doubling against a perfectly-timed backgame:

TIP: Double a backgame when you get down to only three occupied points in front of the two anchors

So Black would not double in diagram 83, but if her next roll were 2-2, clearing the eight-point and seven-point, she would double next roll, regardless of her opponent's reply.

If your opponent has suspect timing, for example fewer than 30 spare pips when you cannot leave a shot next turn, then this will make the position a double. Take the following:

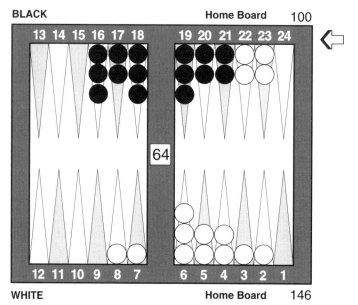

Diag. 86

White's timing is just too fragile to take. Black has no blotting numbers next turn. Even 5-5 and 4-4, normally the nemesis of a player defending against a backgame, both play. White, however, would not be happy to roll either of these. Black should double, and White has a clear pass.

Redoubling

Of course, if we accept the cube when playing a backgame, we hope that we are at least going to get a shot. Usually, but not always, it will be a double shot, in that either of two numbers will hit. If Black rolls a 6-5 in diagram 83 on page 89 she is forced to play 7/1 6/1. We then hit with all fours and fives. However, it would be premature to make an initial double, and we certainly would not redouble if we owned the cube on 2. The basic rule for the backgame player deciding when to double:

WARNING: In a backgame hit your shot first, then think of doubling. You still have to contain the checker you hit

'But surely she will not accept a double after I hit her,' you protest. That depends on a number of factors:

a) how well-placed you are to contain the hit checker.

b) how many checkers she has removed when you hit her.

c) whether there is any chance of your hitting a second checker or jolting one loose.

It is rare that you double or redouble before hitting your shot from a backgame. If you have a quadruple shot which will pretty much win if you hit it, that would just about fit the bill!

Different Anchors

A lot has been written about the value of different anchors in backgames. 'The 5-1 backgame is no good at all,' is one oft-quoted simplification, referring to the backgame player having anchors on the opponent's five-point and ace-point.

Indeed there are significant differences between the various backgames, but these are not as important as matters such as timing, gaps and distribution. Let us consider our well-timed backgame of diagram 83 and move White's anchors around to see what difference it makes.

Firstly, let us see what happens if we give White his opponent's five-point and four-point. In diagram 87 overleaf a double is again premature for Black. She should wait to clear her ten-point and nine-point first. To compare the various backgames we have amended the position so that there is a five-point prime in front of the two anchors, and no gaps for the opponent of the backgame player. For the 5-1 backgame, where there are not enough checkers to do this, we have to content ourselves with a four-prime. In each case we have tried to make the other features of the position the same.

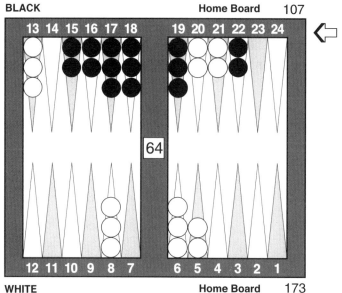

Diag. 87

Computer roll-outs from the world-class computer program Snowie 3 give estimates of the average number of points lost per game for each backgame, and the correct cube action.

Backgame	Points Lost	Cube Action
5-4	0.88	Double, Take
5-3	0.86	Double, Take
5-2	0.80	No Double, Take
5-1	1.24	Double, Pass
4-3	0.56	No Double, Take
4-2	0.71	No Double, Take
4-1	0.94	Double, Take
3-2	0.58	No Double, Take
3-1	0.80	No Double, Take
2-1	1.03	Double, Pass

We can see that the best backgames involve an anchor on the three-point and the worst are when you have the ace-point. In the latter you rarely have good enough timing as your opponent is often slowed down by not having to play sixes. Changing the timing, or any other aspect of the positions, can radically affect the figures. For example, if we increase the timing for the 2-1 backgame still further, to a race deficit of around 150 pips, it becomes 'no double, take'.

'Super Backgames'

Positions in which you have three or four anchors in the opposing board, and excellent timing, we shall term 'super-backgames'. The opponent has great difficulty in bringing his checkers in against the anchors. However, there are so many checkers in the opposing half of the board that it is difficult to contain hit checkers. The winning technique is to build a prime on the other side of the board, and then slowly but surely to roll it forward. These positions have been misassessed by even the strongest computer programs and are uncharted territory for most players. An example:

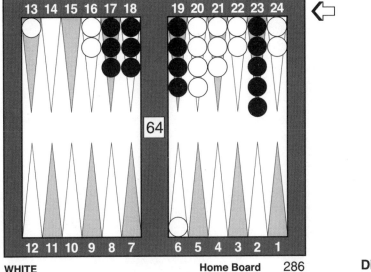

Diag. 88

White is a big favourite here, although the computers don't think so. They think Black is a clear, but not a doubling, favourite. Black is likely to leave triple or quadruple shots as she clears her eight-point and seven-point. White will vacate the 20-point as soon as he can to enable Black to play threes. White is winning the position around 75% of the time, and at double match-point, where gammons are of no value, his strategy will have been justified.

The defence against the type of super-backgame seen above is to avoid hitting too many checkers. If you can split the opposing force in two, this can be deadly.

Exercise 19: Should White double? Should Black take?

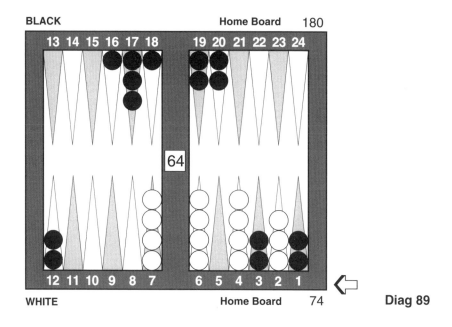

Diag 89

Exercise 20: White is playing a backgame here. How should he play a roll of 1-1?

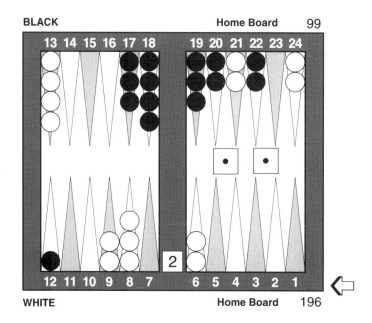

Diag 90

Chapter Eleven

Technical Themes

- **Duplication**
- **Diversification**
- **Going for Gammon**
- **Saving the Gammon**
- **Closed Boards and the Cube**
- **Match Play and Money Play**

Duplication

You will always have to take risks in backgammon. The successful player is the one who minimises those risks, and duplication is a strategy whereby you reduce the good rolls for the opponent. The term is used to describe a situation where you allow your opponent two or more good rolls, but they each involve the same number on one or both dice. If that number is not rolled, then the opponent has many fewer good moves. Let us look at an example:

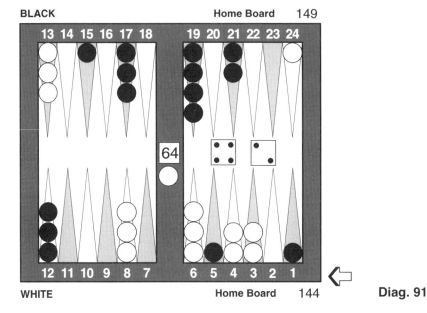

Diag. 91

White is forced to enter with the two, b/23. The four should be played constructively with 13/9, even though it gives Black a direct shot with any four. This uses duplication, in that Black also needs a four to make White's five-point. Of the alternatives, 24/20 is bad, as this gives Black fives, threes and ones to hit, and fours to make the 20-point. 8/4 is solid but passive.

Another example of the theme of duplication often occurs when you are forced to leave a direct shot in a position where you do not want to be hit. If the opponent has a blot in his board, you want to minimise the number of rolls for your opponent which will both hit and cover a blot:

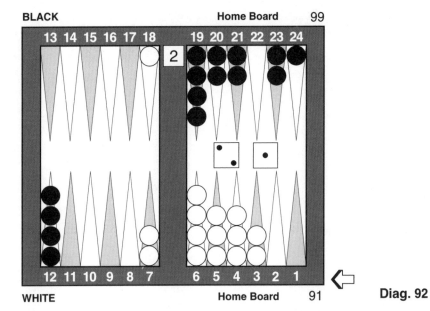

Diag. 92

Here White has rolled a disappointing number; he was hoping to break contact by rolling more than six pips. Now he is forced to leave a direct shot. The general rule is that if you have to leave a direct shot, you should move as close as possible to the checker which can hit you. This is even more true when you lead in the race, and therefore want to break contact. The table of the chances of hitting each of the possible direct shots shows this:

Distance Away	Chance of Hitting	
1	11/36	31%
2	12/36	33%
3	14/36	39%
4	15/36	42%
5	15/36	42%
6	17/36	47%

It would seem, therefore, that White should move to the 15-point, leaving a three shot, but, taking advantage of duplication, the correct play is in fact 18/17 4/2. Black then needs a five to hit and a five to cover his blot on the ace-point, so that 5-5 is the only roll that does both. If, instead, White plays 18/15, then both 3-3 and 5-3 will hit and cover, three rolls instead of one, trebling the risk.

Diversification

If duplication is minimising your opponent's good replies, then diversification is maximising your own good rolls next turn.

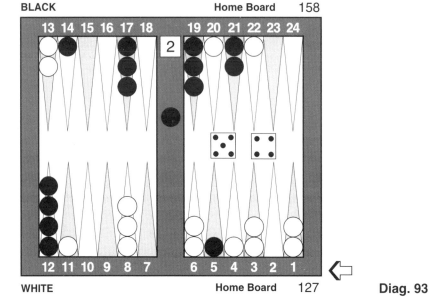

Diag. 93

White is conducting a blitz here and has already doubled. Now he rolls 5-4. Following our advice in Chapter Eight, White should use the four to cover the checker on his four-point, making an extra home-board point. The five should be played 11/6. Currently sixes can be used to hit checkers both on White's 14-point and White's five-point. By moving 11/6, White diversifies good numbers, so that he now has ones and sixes to hit. And, if Black enters on the deuce-point, White will have fours to hit there, a different number again.

Going for Gammon

Sometimes you get a position where you are an overwhelming favourite. You build a six-prime and trap one or more of the opponent's checkers behind it. This is not the time to be doubling, unless you are playing a money game and the cube has not yet been turned. Then, because of the Jacoby Rule you have no alternative but to double and your opponent will pass. This is known as doubling your opponent out, or 'cashing'. In all other cases, you should play on for a possible gammon. Take into account, however, this rule:

NOTE: If you play on for a gammon instead of doubling your opponent out, you need to win two gammons for every loss you incur

This is illustrated by the following position:

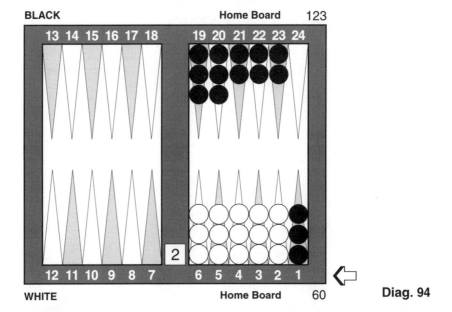

Diag. 94

Black doubled White many moons ago, and now if White offers the cube back on four, Black should drop it like a hot potato. However, White will win quite a few gammons if he plays on. Annoyingly, he will also sometimes leave a shot, be hit, and go on to lose. However, it is always correct to play on against an ace-point anchor. The following is a table of gammons (G) backgammons (BG) and plain-game losses (L) for different numbers of checkers on the ace-point.

Checkers	G	BG	L
1	3%	0%	5%
2	15%	1%	11%
3	32%	3%	14%
4	47%	8%	16%
5	55%	12%	14%

The reader may wonder why it is correct to play on against two checkers on the ace-point, even though the gammon wins are not twice the losses. The reason is that you still have the opportunity to use the cube later if things get sticky.

Another type of position in which it is correct to play for a gammon is when you have a six-prime with one opposing checker trapped behind it.

TIP: The technique for winning a gammon is often to try to pick up a second checker

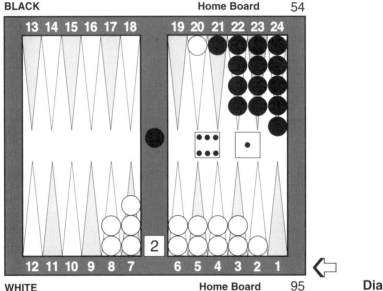

Diag. 95

Here many would cover with the six and look around for the one. The correct play, however, is to volunteer a double shot with 7/1 20/19. If Black does hit, and 20 of her 36 rolls do so, White will usually get a shot at the blot on Black's four-point. White is very unlikely to lose the game, as he can double when all hope of picking up a second checker has gone.

Saving the Gammon

There are some important general rules to follow when you cannot win the game and your sole aim is to save the gammon by getting your stragglers into your home board.

a) Do not waste pips. It is nearly always wrong to move a checker to your four-point or lower. Often it is wrong to waste even one pip by moving a checker to your five-point.

b) Do move a checker to your six-point if possible. That checker is now home and does not need to move again.

c) Cross over from one quadrant to another if you have a choice of plays in the outfield.

d) Avoid having two or more checkers on a particular point, unless you need a particular double and this is the only way to try for it.

e) If you are very unlikely to save the gammon, try to make as many large doubles as possible work for you. If you are almost certain to save the gammon, look out for rolls that surprisingly don't work. For example:

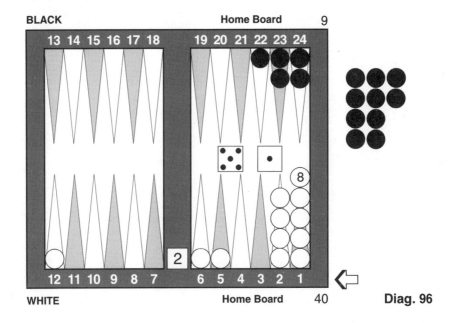

Diag. 96

If White blindly follows the above rules he will play 12/6. Most of the time this will be good enough to save the gammon. The rare times when White's next roll is 4-3 and Black gets a double herself, it won't be good enough. Instead, the careful 12/7 2/1 guarantees saving the gammon.

Closed Boards and the Cube

When you have a closed board and the opponent has one or more checkers on the bar, whether to double or take depends on four factors:

a) the number of checkers on the bar.

b) how many checkers have been borne off.

c) on which points the other checkers are.

d) where the three spare checkers are located.

One checker closed out

The general rule here is that you need to have borne off five checkers and have all your remaining checkers on the one- and two-points to accept a double.

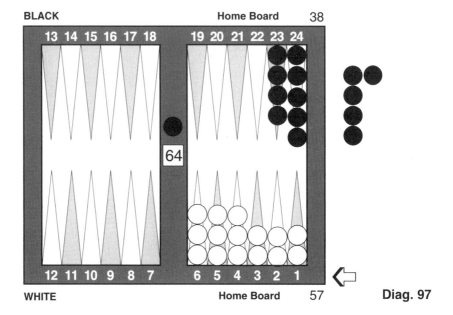

Diag. 97

White has a marginal double in the above position and Black has a clear take. If Black has borne off six checkers (for example removing one checker from Black's ace-point in the diagram 97), White should not double, and Black has a very easy take. Add a checker to Black's two-point and it is a big pass.

It is worth noting here that White's position, with the spare checkers on the six-, five- and four-points, is as good as it could be. The winning chances for White decrease if these checkers are moved to lower points. And if White has an open point, this favours Black considerably.

For the player with the checker on the bar to double, she needs to have borne off more than ten checkers, as in diagram 98 on the next page.

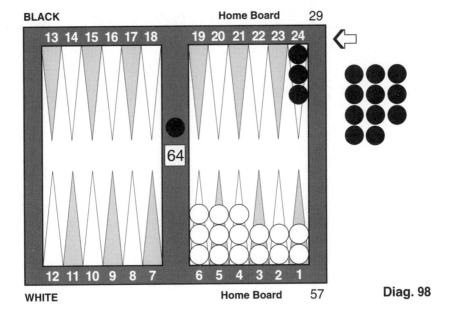

Diag. 98

The above is an example of an optional double by Black and an easy take for White. Adding a black checker to her ace-point means that Black should not double. Removing one means that Black should double and White should pass.

Two checkers closed out
The only question here is how many checkers a player needs to have borne off to accept the cube:

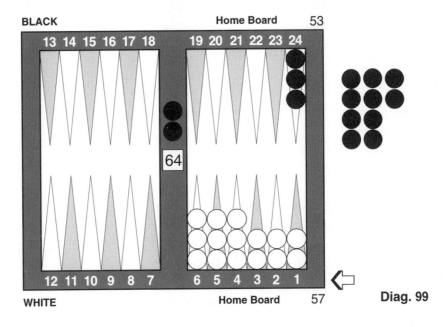

Diag. 99

White should double and Black has a big pass. Removing one checker from Black's ace-point makes the position a marginal double and easy take. If the spare checkers were less well-placed the assessment would change.

When gammons are possible

In our previous positions, the player with the checker(s) closed out could not lose a gammon as she had already borne off one or more checkers. If she has not done so, then a gammon is possible, and the player with the closed board is always too good to double or redouble (other than when the Jacoby rule comes into play). The chance of winning a gammon is almost entirely a function of the number of checkers closed out. Other factors such as the distribution of spare checkers and the opponent's board strength do play a part, but they are insignificant compared with the number of checkers closed out. The jump in the gammon rate for closing out the second and third checkers is significant.

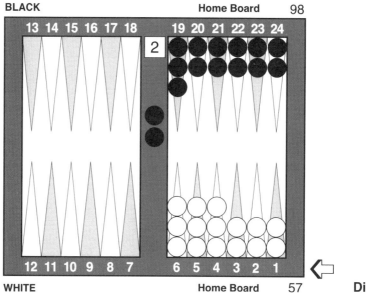

Diag. 100

Here 44% of games are gammon wins for White (including 1% backgammons). Move one of the checkers currently on the bar to Black's six-point, and White only wins 4% gammons. Move a checker from Black's six-point, so that Black has three checkers on the bar, and the percentage of gammons goes up to 79% (including 8% backgammons).

The table of gammons (G), backgammons (BG) and plain-game losses (L) for from one to five checkers closed out shows the gains from hitting extra checkers:

Checkers on bar	G	BG	L
1	4%	0%	2.3%
2	43%	1%	5.2%
3	71%	8%	5.7%
4	65%	22%	6.1%
5	43%	42%	6.7%

It can be seen that losses go up slightly as more checkers are closed out. They nearly all occur when White is forced to leave a shot and gets hit. The gammon rate climbs steadily, and then the backgammon rate starts to climb. So you should usually hit as many checkers as you can.

Money Play and Match Play

There is often a difference between games played for money and games played as part of a tournament match. Money games are played either head-to-head or in chouettes. In the former, you play against one opponent. In the latter, one person (the box), plays against several players (the team), including one captain who makes the decisions on checker plays. Each member of the team has his own cube and takes his own cube decisions. There will be local rules governing many factors such as whether the box can take a partner, and whether the box must double all opponents together, as well as rules on when consultation can take place among the team members.

In match play, the first player to reach a specified number of points is the winner. In an 11-point match, therefore, there is no point in winning a gammon when you have ten points.

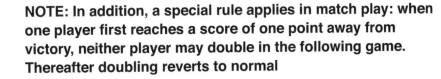

NOTE: In addition, a special rule applies in match play: when one player first reaches a score of one point away from victory, neither player may double in the following game. Thereafter doubling reverts to normal

This is known as the Crawford Rule, and was invented by the renowned American bridge and backgammon expert John R Crawford. It means that the trailer should double immediately in the game after the Crawford game.

One of the unusual effects of this immediate doubling is to create some surprising cube decisions which mystify the beginner. Take the following position, in which White has rolled 3-1 and Black has rolled 2-1, played 24/23 13/11:

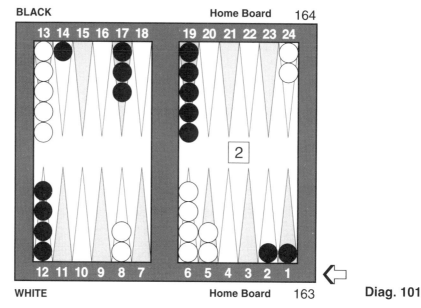

Diag. 101

a) White trails 9-10 in a match to 11
b) White trails 8-10 in a match to 11

White has a small but significant advantage. If it is the Crawford game (Black having won the last game), then he is not allowed to double. If, however, the Crawford game has gone, he should double immediately. Now, if the score is 9-10, Black should pass, and start the next game at even money in the match, rather than play this game as an underdog. If the score is 8-10, however, she should accept. If Black passes, White will still double immediately next game, and will only have to win one more game. If Black takes, then White usually has to win this and the next game.

One other important point is gammons. If White trails 8-10 and doubles, then he will benefit from a gammon, which will mean he wins the match rather than goes level at 10-10. The player one point from victory, however, never benefits from a gammon win. Good match players are always aware of the relevance or otherwise of gammons at all stages of a match.

Exercise 21: Should White double? Should Black take?

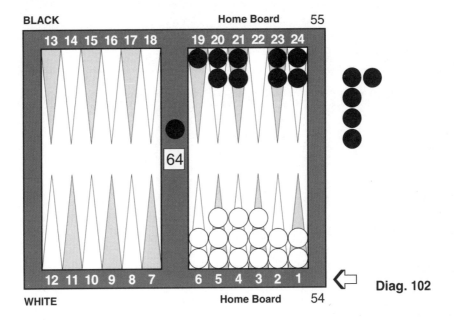

Diag. 102

Exercise 22: One-point match. White to play 1-1

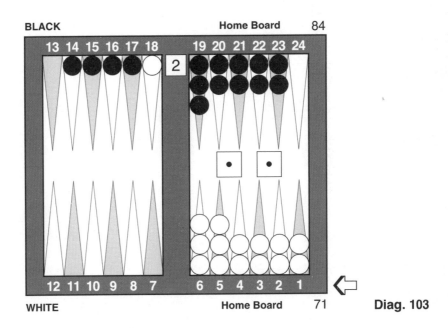

Diag. 103

Chapter Twelve

Computers and the Internet

- ■ **Using Computers to Improve**
- ■ **Internet Servers**
- ■ **Internet Sites**
- ■ **Suppliers**

Using Computers to Improve

Backgammon computers share the status of chess computers as among the very best players in the world. Indeed the two strongest commercially available models, Snowie and Jellyfish, have regularly been among the highest rated players on the main Internet servers. There are two main ways to improve by using a backgammon computer:

a) Play against the computer and ask it to evaluate your moves as you go along, or at the end of the game.

b) Play against human opponents and then ask the backgammon computer to analyse your game.

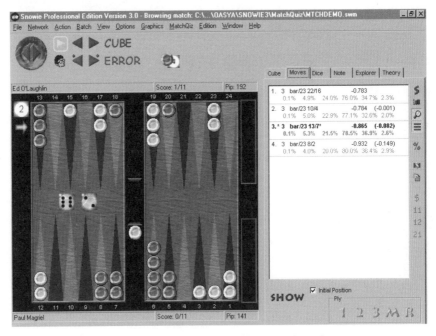

The information-packed Snowie interface

Modern technology, particularly using the Internet servers, allows the recording of backgammon games without any effort. Both Snowie and Jellyfish accept this data easily, and analyse a game while you make a coffee, or an entire match in about ten minutes. As a learning tool, however, Snowie is the better of the two, and offers a wider range of functions. It highlights your blunders, assesses how lucky you were, and even insults you by describing your play as novice level.

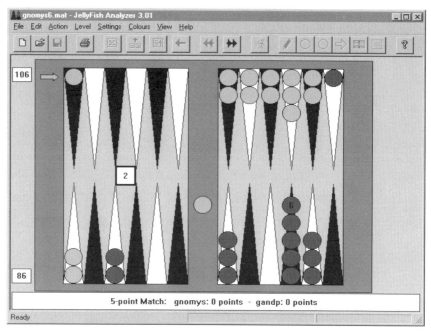

The simple but elegant Jellyfish interface

Sometimes you disagree with its assessment and can ask it to roll out the position, playing maybe a thousand games from the disputed position. Both Snowie and Jellyfish offer this facility, but the former offers a greater variety of ways to do so.

Comparing features of the two programs, there are a number of pleasant but not crucial features of Snowie, such as a wider choice of board designs. However, it is in the area of presentation of data that Snowie comes out on top and the graphs which show your errors and your progress from match to match are invaluable.

If you do decide to buy a top computer program, and you want to use it to analyse your games, then you will need the full program in either case. Snowie 3.2 is the current version and its Professional edition costs $380 (it is priced in dollars, and, at the time of writing, £260 is the sterling price). Jellyfish 3.5 Analyser is the full program, and this retails for £136. Both are available from the suppliers on page 117.

For Snowie you will need at least an i486 processor (Pentium recommended) with 32MB Ram and 90MB HD space. (Jellyfish needs a lot less than this).

Some tips on using backgammon computers

If you just want to have an opponent who will play at any time, and nothing more, then you can obtain cheaper versions of both programs. Jellyfish has a Player and a Tutor version, and Snowie has a Student version. However, none of these allows you to analyse your games.

If you are going to make the best use of a backgammon computer, you should go through every game you play against the computer and every game you can record, such as those you play on the Internet, to discover your errors and find what the computer thought was best. It is in this area that Snowie is without equal, pinpointing your errors and blunders, so that you do not need to look at all the moves you played correctly.

 TIP: The best time to analyse a game is immediately afterwards, when it is still fresh in your mind

Of course you may still be mystified why your chosen move is ranked 27th out of 28 legal moves. Here a strong player can help, and the suppliers on page 117 can put you in touch with professionals in your country who offer tuition at reasonable rates. They can look at printouts from Snowie and come up with remarks such as, 'You shouldn't leave a blot at all here, as your opponent has a five-point board.'

Work you can do to improve

Another way to become stronger is to build up a library of positions you know and understand. You can set up and roll out 50 positions overnight on any reasonably fast computer. In the morning you will have an accurate estimate of the winning chances in each position.

You can also purchase a number of matches between strong players, called MatchQiz and annotated by Kit Woolsey. They are in Snowie format and are pre-loaded (you buy a registration code). Details are on the Snowie site at www.oasya.com.

Unless you are a complete nerd, you will probably want to venture into the outside world and meet the occasional human opponent face-to-face. Record a few interesting positions and analyse them afterwards. Unfortunately, recording all your moves in backgammon is rarely convenient, as it does slow down the play somewhat.

Internet Servers

There are a number of servers that offer on-line backgammon where you can play against opponents from all over the world. Unlike the good old days of Telnet and programs such as Winsoc, logging in and downloading an interface is now easy. The following section takes a look at the pluses and minuses of the main servers (all of which run a rating list and have a facility to save games).

www.fibs.com

FIBS, the First Internet Backgammon Server, is still the best free site. The vast majority of players are very friendly, but FIBS does attract the occasional bad apple. A very high percentage of the players speak English, and the chat is lively if occasionally over the top. The best playing interface is shareware called BBGT, from www.gamercafe.com.

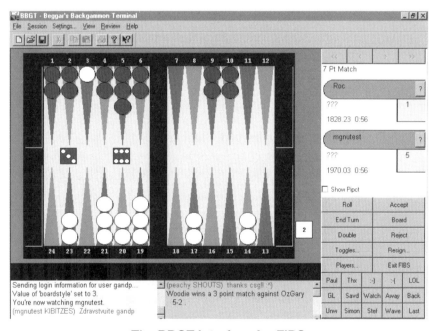

The BBGT interface for FIBS

www.gamesgrid.com

This commercial site is used by most of the top players in the world including Nack Ballard, Kit Woolsey and Paul Magriel. There is an annual charge, currently $80, and regular jackpot tournaments are organised, from which the organisers take a

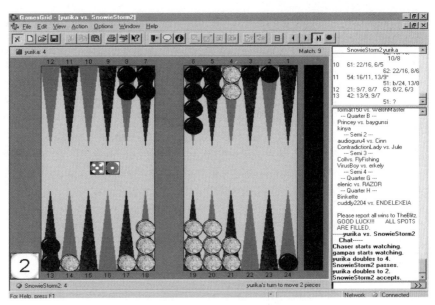

The GamesGrid interface

small percentage. The site has its own excellent interface, and players can and do safely play for money by lodging funds with an online 'banking facility.' There is also a shop which stocks equipment and books.

www.netgammon.com

Maybe the largest site, with a high percentage of French and Turkish players. It is more social than the above two, and again it has its own interface. Regular tournaments are held, and the site has profiles and photographs of the players, and discourages droppers by forcing you to play a move in any unfinished game when you log in. The annual charge is $50.

www.vog.ru

One of the friendliest sites, which also offers a wide range of exotic backgammon variants such as Tapa, Narde (Feuga) and Crazy Narde (Gul Bara), for those who like to try another game for an hour after a disastrous loss. Indeed tournaments are held in all the backgammon variants. The site holds a tourney every few hours, has team events, and stores profiles and photographs of the players. The software occasionally has bugs and server crashes can be irritating, especially if a match one is winning disappears into a black hole in cyberspace. Again there is an annual charge, currently $30, although you can play unrated games without joining.

There are a number of other sites and no doubt a few more will spring up while this book is in production. The ones the author has visited include Yahoo Games (http://games.yahoo.com), the MSN Gaming Zone (www.zone.com/backgammon), GameSite2000 (www.gamesite2000.com/backgammon), Funcom (www.funcom.com), and many other multi-game servers. Not all offer the opportunity to save games or a reliable rating list, but are fine for social play, and all except GameSite2000 are free at the time of writing. This last is the best of the servers on this page, and the interface is excellent. A comprehensive list of servers can be found at the regularly updated site at www.chicagopoint.com.

Internet Sites

The net surfer with an interest in backgammon may no doubt be aware of most of the top sites already. Art Grater's amazing portal at www.back-gammon.com is a good place to start. Another fine site, the Chicago Point Links page at www.chicagopoint.com/links, categorises sites by their main purpose, such as servers or clubs. Both contain a calendar of major tournaments. Another very good site, which also supports Java, is Salar's Backgammon Links at http://salnet.demon.co.uk/backgammon/links. Finally, the site at www.bg-info.com is the expected mine of information and includes some good photographs.

For interesting articles there are several top quality sites. Gammon Village at www.gammonvillage.com has regular interesting features including a lively forum. The Mind Sports Olympiad site at www.msoworld.com has a good backgammon section with a number of theoretical articles within a site which covers all mind games including chess and bridge. Kit Woolsey's site at www.gammonline.com also regularly includes useful theoretical articles, and benefits from having a top player in charge, although there is an annual subscription fee, currently $36.

Free computer software is available on numerous sites on the Internet. One of the better computer programs is Monte Carlo, and a free version which plays one-point matches can be downloaded from www.gamercafe.com. Snowie software can be found at www.oasya.com and a free-trial version of Snowie can be downloaded. Jellyfish software is described in more detail at http://jelly.effect.no/. Hugh Sconyers' backgammon software is available at $99 per CD-ROM from the suppliers below.

Suppliers

Many suppliers of equipment, books and software also have sites on the Internet. Some recommended ones are:

Carol Joy Cole, Flint Area Backgammon Club, 3719 Greenbrook Lane, Flint, MI 48507-1400 USA; tel/fax: (810) 232 9731; email: cjc@tir.com; web site: http://homepage.interaccess.com/~chipoint/Boutique.html

Michael Crane, BIBA, 2 Redbourne Drive, Lincoln LN2 2HG; tel: (01522) 888676; email: info@backgammon-biba.co.uk. web site: www.backgammon-biba.co.uk

Martin de Bruin, Publisher, European Backgammon News, Suite 6/202, P O Box 561, 1/5 Irish Town, Gibraltar; tel/fax: (+34) 950 133009; email: backgammon@bitmailer.net

A&K Klassische Spiele, Grüner Weg 14, 34117 Kassel, Germany; web site: http://www.shopit.de/ak_spiele/frame-e.htm Sets and boards for all classic games..

Backgammon Shop, Dansk Backgammon Forlag ApS, Gersonsvej 25, DK-2900 Hellerup, Denmark; tel: (+45) 3940 1785; fax: (+45) 3940 0144; email: ct@bgshop.com; web site: www.bgshop.com.

The last-named has many out-of-print titles, but the best source of rare books and old backgammon boards on the Internet is the auction at www.ebay.com. The keen purchaser has to be prepared to compete with other buyers, however, and it can help to wake up at 3.59 am to get a final bid in at the close of an auction.

One can often buy a first edition of Magriel's Backgammon on ebay

Solutions to Exercises

1 If you did not reach the position correctly, check the following:

a) that the starting position was correctly set up.

b) that you moved clockwise for Black and anti-clockwise for White.

c) that the first move of the game was made by White.

d) that when you hit a checker, you placed it on the bar.

e) that, for the double, you played four separate threes.

2 There are three legal moves. They are as follows: 5/o 3/o, 5/o 4/1 and 5/2 4/o. Note that you do not have to bear off and you can play either number first, but you must always play both parts of the dice roll if you can.

3 The correct play is b/21 24/21 (diagram 104) making the opponent's four-point. This is better than b/21 8/5* which fights for the five-point but leaves three blots scattered around the board.

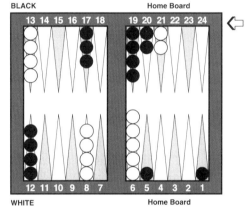

Diag. 104

4 Here the correct play is 24/14*, hitting a Black checker and sending it to the bar. The alternative plays 10/4 8/4 and 13/7 11/7, which make new points, are both good, but hitting a checker is better.

5 The correct play is to hit two checkers with 6/4*/1*. In the opening, hitting two checkers is usually a good idea, and you should do this if you cannot make a new point.

6 The correct play is to make the five-point with 8/5 6/5. This is stronger than hitting on the seven-point, and much better than any move of the back checker. The five-point is vital!

7 White has the advantage in position, as he has a Black checker behind a five-prime. However, he trails in the race, and cannot immediately make a six-prime or close out the Black checker. White should therefore not double and Black has an easy take.

8 Here White's position is too strong to redouble, and Black should pass if White doubles. It is true that White may leave a shot with 6-1 or 5-1, but even then Black is not a favourite to hit it. However, as soon as White clears the two checkers on the six-point he is very likely to win a gammon as Black tries to get her nine outfield checkers into her home board. So: Too Good to Redouble/Pass.

9 The race is White: 97 pips, Black: 105 pips. This is a lead of eight pips, which is a little over 8% of White's pip-count. Therefore White should not double and Black should accept if doubled.

10 Here White has a pip count of 62. He has no penalty at all for gaps or other wastage. Black has four extra cross-overs, costing herself two pips, two surplus checkers on the ace-point — a four pip penalty — and a gap on the four-point for which we also add four pips. The total penalty pips are ten, making the adjusted pip count 62-70, a lead of eight pips, which is more than $12^1/2$% of 62. Therefore White should double and Black should pass.

11 White is not a favourite to get off next roll, whereas Black is, but White only trails by two in the pip-count. Therefore White should double and Black should take.

12 With the four, White should bear off a checker from the four-point. With the three, White cannot bear off. He can fill a gap with 4/1, but that creates a new gap, so the correct play is to play 6/3 which fills a gap, rather than 5/2 which doesn't. (diagram 105)

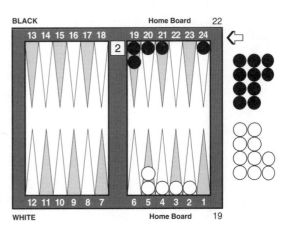

Diag. 105

13 White should play 24/21, which gets to the edge of Black's prime, and 11/9, which covers the blot and makes a five-prime, preventing Black from escaping with sixes. This play is stronger than making the 21-point with 24/21 23/21 or making the four-point with 7/4 6/4.

TIP: If you can do good things on both sides of the board, it is usually better than doing a good thing on only one side of the board.

14 White is threatening to jump with any six but this does not necessarily win. If he does not get it, then he may have to break his six-prime, and Black can then jump herself with a six, or attack on her three-point. White should not double yet and Black has an easy take. A five-prime is often enough compensation for being trapped behind a six-prime.

15 White has only a two-point board but will probably cover the blot on his five-point next roll. However, this is not a game-winning threat. White has some advantage in all three areas, position, race and threats, which is enough to double, but Black should accept. White may well play a blitz here by attacking on his three-point, but all is not lost for Black.

16 White can hit another checker on his 15-point, hit on the ace-point and bring a builder down with the six, or just cover the blot to make the four-point. The last of these options (diagram 106) is much the strongest. If Black does not get an ace in reply she will be in deep trouble.

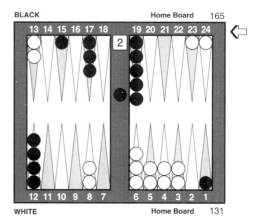

Diag. 106

17 Black is 11 pips down in the race, which it is easy to work out is 11% of White's pip count. This would be a double and take in a race, but Black may also hit a shot, so that it is slightly premature for White to double here. He needs to gain a bit in the race or clear one or two outside points first.

18 White should switch anchors with 20/18(2). He will then get a direct shot as soon as Black is forced to leave her mid-point with a six. Covering the checker on the two-point makes sense with one of the other twos, and 3/1 is correct with the last two. 7/5 would be a clear error, as White wants to keep that spare six, so that he is not forced to break anchor first.

19 White has only three points to clear in front of Black's anchors, but the gap on his five-point is a serious liability. White should not double until the position improves substantially, and Black has an easy take.

20 Currently White is playing a 4-1 backgame, as his anchors are on his opponent's four-point and one-point. The correct plan is to switch to the better 4-2 backgame with 24/23(2). White should hit with the ace 13/12*, as he may contain the Black checker if he is lucky, and the last ace should be played 8/7, starting a point that White very much wants to make. (diagram 107)

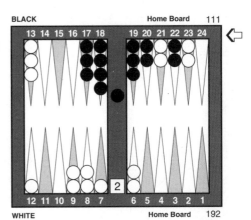

Diag. 107

21 White should double and Black should pass. Although Black has borne off five checkers, her remaining ones are not all on the ace-point and deuce-point, which would be necessary for her to accept the cube. White's spare checkers are not all on the top three points, but the difference is minimal.

22 If we look at the table of losses with one or more checkers closed out on page 107, we see that White should hit one checker but not more than one checker. The correct play is therefore 18/17* 6/3. Moving from White's six-point means that White is not forced to leave a blot with 6-6 next roll.

Probability Tables

There are a number of tables which are useful for players to learn. Firstly, we give the chances to the nearest percentage of hitting a shot more than six pips away (the figures for one to six pips were given on page 99):

Pips Away	Chance of Hitting	
7	6/36	17%
8	6/36	17%
9	5/36	14%
10	3/36	8%
11	2/36	6%
12	3/36	8%
15	1/36	3%
16	1/36	3%
18	1/36	3%
20	1/36	3%
24	1/36	3%

Another helpful table shows the chances of entering from the bar in from one to five rolls (to the nearest percentage) when the opponent has from one to five points made in his board:

Points	1 Roll	2 Rolls	3 Rolls	4 Rolls	5 Rolls
1	97%	100%	100%	100%	100%
2	89%	99%	100%	100%	100%
3	75%	94%	98%	100%	100%
4	56%	80%	91%	96%	98%
5	31%	52%	67%	77%	84%

A final chart which is of benefit, particularly as most matches played on the Internet are from one to five points, shows the approximate chances of winning a match at various scores. These assume both players are of equal ability:

Chances at different scores in a 5-point match

0-0	50%	0-1	42%	0-2	34%	0-3	25%	0-4	15%
1-0	58%	1-1	50%	1-2	41%	1-3	32%	1-4	17%
2-0	66%	2-1	59%	2-2	50%	2-3	40%	2-4	25%
3-0	75%	3-1	68%	3-2	60%	3-3	50%	3-4	30%
4-0	85%	4-1	83%	4-2	75%	4-3	70%	4-4	50%

One often takes these percentages into account when deciding whether to take a cube in a match.

Bibliography

The following books, in approximate order of difficulty, are recommended reading for anyone wishing to improve:

The Backgammon Book by Oswald Jacoby and John R Crawford

Backgammon by Paul Magriel

Backgammon for Serious Players by Bill Robertie

Backgammon: An Independent View by Chris Bray

501 Essential Backgammon Problems by Bill Robertie

Backgammon for Profit by Joe Dwek

100 Backgammon Puzzles by Paul Lamford

Joe Sylvester v Nack Ballard by Kit Woolsey

Philip Marmorstein v Michael Greiner by Kit Woolsey

Mika Lidov v Hal Heinrich by Kit Woolsey

World Class Backgammon Move by Move by Roy Friedman

Advanced Backgammon, vol. 1 and 2 by Bill Robertie

New Ideas in Backgammon by Kit Woolsey and Hal Heinrich

Fascinating Backgammon by Antonio Ortega

How to Play Tournament Backgammon by Kit Woolsey

Jerry Grandell: His Most Important Matches by Antonio Ortega and Danny Kleinmann

Cubes and Gammons Near the End of the Match by Antonio Ortega and Danny Kleinmann

All should be available from the suppliers listed on page 117.

An entertaining read if you can find it in a second-hand bookshop (or on ebay) is *Playboy's Book of Backgammon* by Lewis Deyong. Two thought-provoking works by Barclay Cooke are also long out of print: *Paradoxes and Probabilities* and *Backgammon: The Cruelest Game*. Be warned here, however, that modern computer programs have shown that very many of the suggested moves in these books are not the best. They do provide some excellent source material for study, however. Another good book which is worth looking out for in second-hand bookshops is *Backgammon for People Who Hate to Lose* by former World Champion Tim Holland. As you progress in the game, you may want to buy the other excellent books by Danny Kleinmann which are available from the suppliers on page 117.

Glossary

This glossary contains all the terms the player will meet in this book together with many of the colourful expressions the player will encounter if playing backgammon socially or in tournaments.

Ace   A roll of one on a die. Also, the ace-point is the one-point.

Anchor   A point in the opponent's home board, or the opponent's bar-point, occupied by two or more of your checkers.

Automatic Double   By agreement in a money game only, if both players roll the same number on the initial roll, the cube is automatically placed on two, but remains centred.

Backgame   A position in which you have two or more anchors in the opponent's board and aim to hit a shot as he attempts to bring his checkers into his board.

Backgammon The win of three times the value of the cube when the opponent still has one or more checkers in your home board or on the bar and has not borne off a checker.

Baffle Box   A device, whose use is optional, into which dice are thrown when rolling. It contains a helter-skelter of three slopes which ensures that the roll is fair.

Bar   The central dividing area between the two halves of the board, on which hit checkers are placed.

Bar-point   A player's seven-point.

Bear Off   To take a checker off the board in the closing stages; the stage when one or both players have all their checkers in the home board.

Beaver   To double the value of an offered cube while retaining ownership of the cube on your side of the board.

Blot   A single vulnerable checker of either colour occupying a point.

Blitz   An attack on one or more of your opponent's back checkers with the aim of repeatedly sending them to the bar.

Blockade   Any series of points, whether consecutive or not, which prevents the opponent playing particular numbers.

Board   Points made in a player's home board, e.g. a four-point board.

Box   In a chouette, the player who is on his own.

Boxes (in US, Boxcars)   A roll of double sixes.

Broken Prime   A prime with a gap in it.

Builder   A spare checker, usually on one of the points from a player's 11-point to his seven-point, which can be used to make a point in board on a future roll.

Captain   In a chouette, the member of the team who takes the final decision on checker plays.

Centred Cube   One that has not yet been turned in that game, and shows 64, although its real value is one.

Checker   One of the 30 round pieces used for playing the game.

Chouette   A form of money game in which one player (the box) plays against other players (the team) one of whom (the captain) is rolling and making the checker plays. Each player has his own cube and makes his own decisions whether to take or pass.

Close(d) Out   When one or more checkers are on the bar against a six-point home board.

Cocked Die   A die which has not come to rest flat in the player's right-hand side of the board or which is on top of a checker.

Contact   A situation where the possibility of hitting a shot still exists.

Contain   To prevent one or more checkers from escaping from your side of the board by a combination of making blocking points and hitting.

Count   To add up the number of pips required to bear off all the remaining checkers; the total so reached for both sides.

Crash   To be forced to break the six-point and possibly other points in your home board; also termed to crunch.

Crawford Rule   In tournament matches only, the rule by which, in the game immediately after one player reaches a score one point from victory, the cube may not be used.

Crossover   A move from one quarter of the board to another.

Cube   The doubling cube, which starts in the centre of the board and which may be used by either player to increase the value of the game.

Dance   To fail to enter from the bar.

Desmonds   Slang for the roll of double twos. Apparently named after Archbishop Desmond Tutu.

Deuce   A roll of two on a die; the two-point is also known as the deuce-point.

Direct Shot   Any situation where a blot is six or fewer pips away from an opponent's checker.

Diversification   Placing one's checkers such that the maximum number of rolls will play well on the next throw.

Double   Any roll of the same number on each die; any offer of a cube; to offer the cube.

Double Shot   A blot exposed to two different direct shots.

Drop   To reject or pass an offered cube.

Duplication   A situation where one or more of the opponent's rolls offers a choice between different hitting or point-making moves, thus reducing the number of good rolls which the opponent may throw.

Enter   To roll a number corresponding to a point not occupied by two or more of your opponent's checkers and to move the checker from the bar to that point.

Equity   The average expected amount that will be won or lost in that particular game. For example, if you are certain to win a backgammon, your equity is +3.

Fan   American slang for failing to enter from the bar.

Flunk   More American slang for failing to enter from the bar.

Gammon   The win of twice the value of the cube when the opponent has not borne off any checkers, but he has no checkers in your home board or on the bar.

Golden Anchor   The opponent's five-point; your 20-point.

Golden Point   Your five-point.

Hit   To move a checker to a point occupied by only one of your opponent's checkers, thereby sending it to the bar.

Hit Loose   To hit a blot in your home board thereby giving your opponent an opportunity to hit the same checker from the bar.

Holding Game   A situation in which a player has an anchor and is waiting to get a shot or to run with a double.

Home Board   The six points from one to six from which the player bears off.

Indirect shot   Any situation where a blot is seven or more pips away from an opponent's checker, and there is at least one roll of the dice which will allow the opponent to hit it.

Inner Board   The home board.

Jacoby Paradox   A position in the bear-off, with one side having a checker on the five-point and two-point, which is not a redouble if the opponent will offer you a takeable cube when you miss, but is a double if the cube is of no value to your opponent if you miss.

Jacoby Rule   The rule, usually employed in money games, that a gammon or backgammon does not count until an initial double has been made.

Kauder Paradox   A rare position which is a correct double and a correct beaver. It can apply only in a money game.

Latto Paradox   A very rare position, only in a money game, which is a correct redouble but not an initial double.

Lipped Cups Cups that have a ridge at the top to prevent the dice being rolled in an unfair way by a mechanic.

Lover's Leap An opening roll of 6-5 played by moving a checker from the 24-point to the mid-point.

Man A term commonly used for a checker.

Mechanic Someone who can cheat by rolling the dice in such a way that certain numbers appear with a greater frequency than they should. Also known as a dice mechanic.

Mid-point The player's 13-point.

Miss To fail to hit a shot, or, in the bear-off, to roll a number which has to be moved without taking off a checker.

No Dice Slang for a faulty roll or for cocked dice.

Outer Board The area of the board from a player's 12-point to his seven-point.

Outfield Point Any point outside the two home boards.

Outside Prime A sequence of four or more points, none of which is in the player's home board.

Pass To reject an offered cube.

Pick and Pass To hit a blot with one part of the roll and to continue with the same checker to an occupied point.

Pigeon Slang for a weak player who is prepared to play for money against stronger players.

Pip-Count The total number of pips which must be rolled to bring all checkers into the home board and to bear them off.

Point Any of the 24 spikes on which the checkers are placed; more commonly, such a triangle occupied by two or more of a player's checkers. To point on a checker is to move two checkers to the point occupied by an opponent's checker, sending it to the bar.

Precision Dice Dice manufactured with extreme accuracy which have no bias.

Premature Roll A roll made before the opponent has completed his play by picking up his dice.

Prime A sequence of at least four consecutive points each occupied by two or more checkers of the same colour.

Rac(c)oon After an initial double has been beavered, to turn the cube to double its previous value, while allowing the opponent to retain it on his side of the board.

Race A position where all, or virtually all, contact has been broken and the possibility of hitting shots is minimal or non-existent.

Redouble Any double made subsequent to the initial double.

Return A shot from the bar against one of the opponent's checkers immediately after being hit.

Roll-out A means of evaluating the equity of a position by playing a large number of games from that position.

Run To move a back checker into the outer board.

Settlement An agreement to end the game with a certain number of points being paid by one player to one or more others.

Shake To mix the dice using the dice cups prior to rolling; also used as a general term for any roll or throw.

Shift (points) To move both checkers from one point to another, often while hitting a loose blot.

Slot To voluntarily place a blot on an important point with a view to making that point if the blot is not hit.

Snake Eyes A roll of double ones.

Split To move a back checker, occupying an anchor, one or more pips within the opponent's home board or to the opponent's bar-point.

Steaming Taking irrational cube decisions in money games in a desperate attempt to recover previous losses.

Take To accept an offered cube.

Timing A measure of how long one can retain a desired position before being forced to make concessions.

Trap Play To volunteer a direct shot with a view to forcing the opponent to move off an anchor.

Wait To decide not to to double or redouble on the current turn.

Wash A settlement where two or more players agree that no points will be won by either side in this game. It normally occurs when the chances are approximately equal, and sometimes with a high cube.

Weaver To deliberately make an inferior play hoping to get your opponent to accept the cube incorrectly next turn.